SPEAK!
THY SERVANT HEARETH

SPEAK!
THY SERVANT HEARETH

by Dr. John Tetsola

Bogota, New Jersey

Speak! Thy Servant Heareth

An Insight to discerning God's Voice and Understanding His Guidance Systems

 Published by END TIME WAVE PUBLICATIONS, P.O. Box 141, Bogota, New Jersey 07603-0141.

ISBN 0-9634306-9-6

Note: In some Scripture quotations, italics have been added by the author for emphasis only.

Dedication

This book is dedicated to my mother Comfort who has continually been a great source of support and a blessing to me. Mom, you are the best mother anyone can ask for. Thanks for the discipline and the push to excel. I also dedicate this book to my brother Dennis for his strength and tenacity in making sure that I accomplish what God has for my life.

AUTHOR'S PREFACE

We are living in a time and a season that demands a listening ear and an ability to hear the Voice of the Lord. The increase of demonic activity daily bombards and affects every Christian. We are confronted with situations that call for specific instructions to attain or maintain our health, prosperity and well-being in life. We need to know where to live, what to drive, what doctor to trust and which foods to eat. Danger lurks around every corner. Our government's motives are in a cycle of change. Our survival as a people hinges upon our ability to hear the spoken Word of the Lord.

This is not the time to indulge in the pettiness of debate. Too many Christians have attempted to utilize their opinion as law and have created confusion in the Body. Too many have echoed false doctrines and demonic lies that have crippled many. Some of the psychics are people who were prophetically gifted to hear God, yet rejected by the Church through prejudice and lack of understanding. Too many people are missing their purpose because of deafened ears and prejudiced minds. Rejection incubates rebellion, and rebellion enthrones a lie. Theory is not truth, nor is the concept of theology when it defies the written Word of God. The Word of God is our standard, but in this book, your questions concerning the Voice of the Lord will be answered and, prayerfully, you will drop your defenses and develop a living and thriving relationship with the Lord which will develop in you the ability to understand His guidance.

The very word "relationship" carries an inherent implication of communication. To deny God's ability to communicate with man is to deny His ability to relate to man. If God cannot relate to us, then why do we pray? It really wouldn't make much sense for us to pray to a God that could not answer us....we'd be better off talking to a brick wall.

Thankfully, God is real and desires that we experience Him in His multi-dimensional totality.

God desires to become an intimate part of our lives; to share the little problems as well as the crucial ones. He will laugh and cry with us, if we allow Him. He will demonstrate Himself to us when we drop all of our predetermined assessments and open our hearts to receive Him in whatever manner He chooses to correspond with us.

We must become intimate with God and learn His inner parts. For out of this measure of relationship we will be able to hear as He directs our paths. Only the Voice of God can direct us through the crooked places of life. Only the Voice of God can give us insight from our past and wisdom for our future. We must develop an ear that is attuned to His Voice. Let he that hath an ear hear what the Spirit of the Lord is saying in this hour!

John Tetsola, Ph.D.

TABLE OF CONTENTS

CHAPTER I

THE IMPORTANCE OF GOD'S GUIDANCE

For as many as are led by the Spirit of God, they are the sons of God.

Romans 8:14

There was a story about a businessman who was a Christian, but did not spend very much time in the Word. One day he prayed and said, "Lord, I need a word of guidance." Then he let his Bible flip open, closed his eyes and put his finger down on the page. He stopped on the word "wheat." So he called his stockbroker and invested a large sum of money in wheat futures. Within weeks he was prospering and had made a fortune. After a while, he needed another word from the Lord. He took his Bible off the coffee table, let it flip open, closed his eyes and put his finger down. He stopped on the word "oil." Then he called his stockbroker, liquidated all of his wheat stocks and bought oil. He again prospered and began to make a fortune. When things started to go bad in the oil business, instead of getting out, he decided to ride it out. He ended up losing everything. He was devastated. He went to a friend who was an attorney for some advice. His lawyer friend began to advise him about different forms of bankruptcy. He was shocked about the advice and said, "I don't believe God will guide me into this situation." The lawyer said, "Well you'd better get a Word from God, because you are in big trouble." The man then went back home to God and said, "Lord, I have to know what to do in this situation." Then he opened his Bible again, closed his eyes and let it fall open, and just placed his finger on the page. When he opened his eyes, it said "chapter eleven."

Interestingly enough, that is how a lot of believers approach guidance. Either this way or they call a psychic hotline. God's guidance is many-sided in its complexity. Each part is simple, but if you don't have a complete overview of how God guides, you will be misled. You must understand that God can judge you without killing you. He can turn your lights out. When He wanted to judge the nation of Israel, He did not kill or destroy them. He just turned out their lights, and they wandered for forty years. There were motions without direction.

When Cain was judged by God, He did not smite him with a lightning bolt. He became a fugitive and a wanderer. If God wants to curse a church, judge a denomination, a believer or a movement, God can simply turn out the lights. When the light is out and no word of direction is provided, you start wandering and living in confusion. God does not want us to wander. He is not the author of confusion. He is not double-minded. If we are, we will not be able to receive anything from God.

God is training a people who can govern their own lives, who can make appropriate and wise decisions on complex problems, who are not being tossed to and fro by every wind of doctrine and every word. You've got to be mature to do that. You don't have to be mature to go to heaven, but you will have to be mature to succeed in this life. If you are one of those church wanderers, or if your life is, "Well, I just don't know what to do," that is not a blessing. That is a curse. God wants you to know what to do, and He is not out to confuse you. You have to understand and know for yourself how God guides our lives in determining His will and direction. It is very exciting to know that God guides His people and that He does not want you to fail. He wants you to succeed. In the Old Testament, God guided the children of Israel through the wilderness with a cloud by day and a fire by night. God said to the Israelites, when the cloud moves out of the camp, you move. When the cloud remains, you remain. That was pretty easy, and yet some of them missed it. God is saying today in the New Testament that the guidance systems of God have moved inside the believer. It is no longer externalized and physical. It is internalized and spiritual.

THE EXTREMES OF GUIDANCE

There are two extremes in guidance that I must caution you about. First, the extreme of human rationalization. Second, the extreme of mysticism. Both of them are deadly and wrong. Human rationalization is the mentality that never moves outside the realm of what is seen, what is known and what is logical. All questions answered, every door opened, no risk involved, and that is when we decide to move out in faith. The problem with this extreme is that you are only walking by sight and not by faith. Paul says that we walk by faith and not by sight. In our experiences, however, faith is sometimes spelled "risk," but it is calculated risk. It is not presumptuous risk. It is not foolish risk.

The other extreme is mysticism. These kinds of people are led by unseen, unknowable and uncertain nonsense. Their answer for everything is "I feel led." Any time they want an excuse for doing what they want to do anyway, these people say, "I feel led." These kinds of people are disasters waiting to happen. Determine to avoid both extremes. The extreme mystical person moves into the subjective realm and ignores

Scripture and wise counsel, including circumstances. Both of these extremes will get you in trouble.

> **Then Agrippa said unto Paul, Almost thou persuadest me to be a Christian.**
>
> **Acts 26:28**

Here the Apostle Paul is standing before King Agrippa giving testimony as to why he has been in prison. He is preaching the resurrected Christ. King Agrippa was in the human rationalization mode and Paul never got him saved. Finally, in verse 28, Agrippa said "Paul, you almost persuade me to be a Christian." He stayed logical and rational and never got saved. There are many people who are not in the kingdom of God today because of mental hangups. They are too logical and they cannot accept by faith that the unseen God made the world that is seen. It is not rational, so they grasp something more irrational than that.

On the other hand, you have mysticism. In II Kings 5, Naaman the leper went to the prophet Elisha because he had leprosy and had heard that Elisha had a great healing ministry. But Elisha did not heal him like he thought he should. He wanted all the hand waving, all the candle lights, the angelic visitation and the hoopla, or it couldn't be healing. That is a subjective feeling.

> **Therefore I write these things being absent, lest being present I should use sharpness, according to the power which the Lord hath given me to edification, and not to destruction.**
>
> **II Corinthians 13:10**

Paul explains to us the problem with guidance in this Scripture. I think in America today, one of the problems in hearing God is that there are too many voices. We've got to turn off the television and the VCR, put down the newspaper, turn the CD player off and take the phone off the hook just to hear the Voice of God. We need discernment to hear His Voice. Every voice speaking to you is not God. In John 12, the Father spoke from heaven to Christ the Son. Some of the people said it was an angel. Others standing by said it was thunder. They all knew something happened, but only Jesus knew it was the Father's Voice. It takes discernment to hear when God is speaking. In Isaiah 58:11, it says the Lord will guide you continually. This is the promise of the Lord to you. God wants to lead you somewhere. His plans for you are good and not evil.

THE HUNGER OF THE HEART

This is the greatest time in the history of the Church for the Body of Christ to develop the ability to hear what the Spirit of the Lord is saying. Dullness of hearing has become one of our greatest problems, both individually and collectively. Most people erroneously think God is not speaking because they are unable to discern His Voice. Yet there remains a hunger within the hearts of many in the Body of Christ who yearn to know how to hear the Voice of God.

This problem exists because we have not been properly taught the great importance and necessity of hearing from God. I believe from the depth of my heart that once an individual is born again, one of the many things that he or she needs to be taught quickly is how to know or tell when God is leading or speaking to them. He must learn how to discern the Voice of God, his new Father, and understand His guidance system.

There are Christians who have been in the faith for years who remain unable to know when God is speaking and cannot discern or recognize the instrument He is using. This is a great problem among the Body of Christ today. Many have chosen wrong careers, wrong callings and wrong ministries while claiming that God told them to do so. Others have married the wrong man or woman because they were ignorant. They could not discern the Voice of God. As a result of this, many marriages, calls and ministries have been destroyed. There are many believers that have encountered this problem. They need directions for their lives, their ministries and their families, and yet they find it difficult to hear and discern the Voice of God.

The problem is not that God is not speaking. The problem is that God's people have not been properly trained to hear and discern His guidance systems. God is calling for men and women who can identify and understand His Voice.

And the child Samuel ministered unto the LORD before Eli. And the word of the LORD was precious in those days; *there was* no open vision.

And it came to pass at that time, when Eli *was* laid down in his place, and his eyes began to wax dim, *that* he could not see;

And ere the lamp of God went out in the temple of the LORD, where the ark of God *was,* and Samuel was laid down *to sleep;*

That the LORD called Samuel: and he answered, Here *am* I.

And he ran unto Eli, and said, Here *am* I; for thou calledst me. And he said, I called not; lie down again. And he went and lay down.

And the LORD called yet again, Samuel. And Samuel arose and went to Eli, and said, Here *am* I; for thou didst call me. And he answered, I called not, my son; lie down again.

Now Samuel did not yet know the LORD, neither was the word of the LORD yet revealed unto him.

And the LORD called Samuel again the third time. And he arose and went to Eli, and said, Here *am* I; for thou didst call me. And Eli perceived that the LORD had called the child.

Therefore Eli said unto Samuel, Go, lie down: and it shall be, if he call thee, that thou shalt say, Speak, LORD; for thy servant heareth. So Samuel went and lay down in his place.

And the LORD came, and stood, and called as at other times, Samuel, Samuel. Then Samuel answered, Speak; for thy servant heareth.

Samuel 3:1-10

The Bible describes Samuel as a "child." This does not mean that Samuel was a newborn baby, but it actually emphasizes the youthfulness of Samuel in the days of his training under Eli. The Hebrew word for child is "NAAR." It means "a child from the age of infancy to adolescence." The Word of the Lord was precious in the days of Samuel. It was precious in those days because revelations, prophecies, visions and contacts with Jehovah were scarce and therefore valuable.

The Bible also tells us in verse 4 that when Samuel was called by God, Samuel thought that it was Eli calling him. This simply tells us that Samuel did not know how to discern the Voice of God and that he had not been properly taught about hearing the Voice of God. Jehovah spoke to Samuel with an audible Voice so strong that it woke Samuel out of his sleep. Yet, Samuel thought that it was his pastor and mentor,

Eli, calling him. Not only did God speak to Samuel audibly, but God actually came and stood bodily at a certain place. Yet, Samuel was still unable to understand and discern the Voice of God.

This is grievous and pathetic. Many believers in the Body of Christ today are experiencing the same problem that Samuel encountered during his time. We still have men and women who cannot discern the Voice of God from the voice of men. If God would come down in Person and stand in front of some Christians today, they wouldn't recognize or know that He is God. Thankfully, God still speaks and there remain men and women who hear from Him and who can discern His Presence. The Bible tells us that Samuel "did not yet know the Lord, neither was the Word of the Lord yet revealed unto him." Samuel was not acquainted with the way God speaks. He had not been taught by Eli about hearing God's Voice. This was the first time God was speaking to him.

There is a great concern here. Why should it take Samuel three calls from the Lord to make Eli actually realize that God was speaking to the young man? Eli was the leader. He was equivalent to the pastor or the five-fold ministry gifts today. He was the one in charge of mentoring Samuel. Today, there are great expectations placed upon leaders. Many of them fall short of God's expectation. God needs dependable and trustworthy men and women. God is looking for believers who can convey His messages. One would expect that as a leader and mentor, Eli must have known or been taught during his servanthood about discerning and hearing the Voice of God. Yet we see evidence to the contrary in this Scripture.

The great danger here is that there are many Christians, and ministers in particular, that are in this same predicament. They yearn and crave internally and secretly to actually be able to clearly discern and understand God's Voice and leading. But because some of these individuals occupy great offices and positions in the ministry of the Church, some find it degrading, embarrassing and humiliating to acknowledge their lack of discernment and understanding. Many have led God's people astray and many have become redundant and stale because of their failure to understand the leading of God.

Notice what the Bible says. After the third call, Eli perceived that God was speaking to Samuel. It took Eli three occasions to discern that God was speaking to young Samuel. You see, whenever God intends to accomplish a thing, He speaks through His people. But when there is not an available vessel, the Word becomes scarce and precious in that life and in that generation.

GOD'S VOICE FOR CROSSROAD EXPERIENCES

Then they told David, saying, Behold, the Philistines fight against Keilah, and they rob the threshingfloors.

Therefore David inquired of the LORD, saying, Shall I go and smite these Philistines? And the LORD said unto David, Go, and smite the Philistines, and save Keilah.

And David's men said unto him, Behold, we be afraid here in Judah: how much more then if we come to Keilah against the armies of the Philistines?

Then David inquired of the LORD yet again. And the LORD answered him and said, Arise, go down to Keilah: for I will deliver the Philistines into thine hand.

So David and his men went to Keilah, and fought with the Philistines, and brought away their cattle, and smote them with a great slaughter. So David saved the inhabitants of Keilah.

I Samuel 23:1-5

David understood and knew the importance of God's guidance. When the Philistines fought against Keilah and invaded the country to carry off the harvest, David did not panic and rush to battle against the enemy. He instead wanted to know the mind of God. He wanted to know what God had to say concerning the invasion. He needed new direction. David knew that for him to be successful in his exploit, he had to apprehend and employ God's strategy. The Bible lets us know that David inquire of the Lord. To "inquire" means "to ask, seek and examine."

When we begin to learn how to inquire of the Lord before any decisions are made, we will begin to experience a flow of answers from the Presence of God. God is still speaking, but God's people are too lazy to inquire.

Then David inquired of the LORD yet again. And the LORD answered him and said, Arise, go down to Keilah: for I will deliver the Philistines into thine hand.

I Samuel 23:4

Notice the reply of the Lord. The Lord answered David and told him to go to Keilah, for the Philistines would be delivered into his hand. How did David know that it was God speaking to him? Because while he was at the backside of the desert caring for his father's sheep, he was properly trained. He knew and was able to discern and hear the Voice of God. His inquiring of the Lord brought him new direction. David knew how to hear the Voice of the Lord. Thus, he was able to lead God's people to victory. This is essential for the Body of Christ to know. Developing the ability to hear from God will enable ministers to effectively lead God's people in the right direction.

GOD'S VOICE FOR BUSINESS AFFAIRS AND DIRECTIONS

> **And the asses of Kish Saul's father were lost. And Kish said to Saul his son, Take now one of the servants with thee, and arise, go seek the asses.**
>
> **And when they were come to the land of Zuph, Saul said to his servant that was with him, Come, and let us return; lest my father leave caring for the asses, and take thought for us.**
>
> **And he said unto him, Behold now, there is in this city a man of God, and he is an honourable man; all that he saith cometh surely to pass: now let us go thither; peradventure he can show us our way that we should go.**
>
> **I Samuel 9:3,5,6**

The importance of hearing from God was again depicted in Saul's experience. Saul, the son of Kish, was out looking for his father's missing asses. But when he and his servant were unable to find the missing asses, Saul became frustrated and wanted to call off his assignment and mission. Many of us do the same thing today. Just because we are unable to quickly arrive at our destination in God, we become frustrated, depressed and want to give up the call, ministry, and vision of God upon our lives.

> **And he said unto him, Behold now, there is in this city a man of God, and he is an honourable man; all that he saith**

cometh surely to pass: now let us go thither; peradventure he can show us our way that we should go.

I Samuel 9:6

Saul's servant was able to convince and persuade Saul to seek out the man of God. The purpose of visiting the man of God was to hear what God had to say concerning the missing asses. Before this time, Saul was about to give up the search. It took the Word of the Lord to send him in a new direction. Thank God for Saul's servant! We need this type of men today. We need servants that will be able to persuade their master and direct them to the right source where they can hear and receive guidance, if need be.

There are many Christians who are at a crossroad. Some are considering giving up their assignment because they are unable to find the "asses." The Church is in its greatest hour, and God is raising up servants that will direct His people to the right source. They will direct God's people to the place where the asses are found and the place where the anointing is poured.

And as for thine asses that were lost three days ago, set not thy mind on them; for they are found. And on whom is all the desire of Israel? Is it not on thee, and on all thy father's house?

And Saul answered and said, Am not I a Benjamite, of the smallest of the tribes of Israel? and my family the least of all the families of the tribe of Benjamin? wherefore then speakest thou so to me?

And Samuel took Saul and his servant, and brought them into the parlour, and made them sit in the chiefest place among them that were bidden, which were about thirty persons.

I Samuel 9:20-22

Saul decided to inquire what God had to say concerning the missing asses. Not only did God speak to Saul through the prophet Samuel, God also told him what was to become of his life. God was about to promote him. He was about to take him from being an ass searcher to a leader of His people. Many times, we are unable to accomplish an assignment because we don't know the Word of the Lord concerning that situation. We have to seek the Word of the Lord. We need to hear from God.

GOD'S VOICE FOR WARFARE

And Jehoshaphat said unto the king of Israel, Inquire, I pray thee, at the word of the LORD to day.

I Kings 22:5

There is nothing as important as being able to hear and understand God's leading and direction. According to the Scripture, King Ahab desired to reclaim Ramoth in Gilead. Ahab sought the assistance of King Jehoshaphat of Israel to accompany him on the assignment. Jehoshaphat was more concerned about what God had to say concerning the battle than in discovering what King Ahab had in mind. Jehoshaphat wanted to hear from God before anything else. He wanted God's direction. He needed guidance.

You see, hearing from God will change your life. The reason most Christians are still on the old street of defeat is because they have not learned to seek the Word of the Lord for a new path. Jehoshaphat wanted to inquire of the Lord. He wanted to know God's guidance in the battle. He needed to hear something new and fresh from the Throne of God. He wanted to be directed properly.

> **Then the king of Israel gathered the prophets together, about four hundred men, and said unto them, Shall I go against Ramothgilead to battle, or shall I forbear? And they said, Go up; for the Lord shall deliver it into the hand of the king.**
>
> **I Kings 22:6**

Ahab gathered all of his false prophets to prophesy what he wanted to hear. There are a lot of false prophets today, even in the midst of God's true prophets. Listening and receiving the Word of the Lord from these false prophets will send you to an untimely death. They will lead you to battle and watch you die.

> **And Jehoshaphat said, Is there not here a prophet of the LORD besides, that we might inquire of him?**
>
> **I Kings 22:7**

Notice something here. King Jehoshaphat was not comfortable with the words given by Ahab's prophets. Something seemed lacking in the messages of these prophets, so Jehoshaphat asked if there was a prophet of Jehovah in the kingdom, besides these prophets of Baal. Always remember that a wrong word, when not refused, will destroy your destiny. A right word will guard, build and release you. We need to allow the gift of the discerning of spirits to flow through us.

Jehoshaphat requested a true prophet of the Lord because he wanted to hear what God had to say about the war before he made any moves.

> **And the king of Israel said unto Jehoshaphat, There is yet one man, Micaiah the son of Imlah, by whom we may inquire of the LORD: but I hate him; for he doth not prophesy good concerning me, but evil. And Jehoshaphat said, Let not the king say so.**
>
> **I Kings 22:8**

Finally, the prophet Micaiah was brought before the king. Now listen to what King Ahab had to say about prophet Micaiah. "I hate him, for he doth not prophesy good concerning me, but evil." Does this sound familiar? The true prophets of God will not speak and prophesy only what you want to hear. They will only speak what God wants them to say. They will hear from God and speak His Mind and purposes in the earth, for that is their calling. They will cause new wells to be dug in your life.

> **And the messenger that was gone to call Micaiah spake unto him, saying, Behold now, the words of the prophets declare good unto the king with one mouth: let thy word, I pray thee, be like the word of one of them, and speak that which is good.**
>
> **I Kings 22:13**

Even though Micaiah was verbally bribed by Zedekiah, the son of Chenaanah, to speak the same false word as the other prophets of Baal, he refused in the long run and spoke the mind of God concerning the battle at Ramoth in Gilead. That is what the true prophets of God will do. The Church will not be able to bribe them. They will not compromise. They will speak in the midst of adversity and calamity.

And Micaiah said, As the LORD liveth, what the LORD saith unto me, that will I speak.

So he came to the king. And the king said unto him, Micaiah, shall we go against Ramothgilead to battle, or shall we forbear? And he answered him, Go, and prosper: for the LORD shall deliver it into the hand of the king.

I Kings 22:14-1

Did you notice what Micaiah said? He said he would speak only what the Lord told him to speak. Even when he was about to compromise, the king knew it was unlike him, so he adjured Micaiah to speak the truth in the Name of Jehovah. Micaiah knew that this was what Ahab wanted to hear, even though it was not a true message. Micaiah intended to see what Ahab would do if he did agree with the false prophets. Knowing that it was not genuine, Ahab pressed him further for the truth, even though it did not harmonize with the words spoken by the prophets of Baal. You can see the great need for the Body of Christ to be taught properly about God's guidance system.

GOD'S VOICE FOR EMERGENCIES

Thy father made our yoke grievous: now therefore make thou the grievous service of thy father, and his heavy yoke which he put upon us, lighter, and we will serve thee.

And he said unto them, Depart yet for three days, then come again to me. And the people departed.

And king Rehoboam consulted with the old men, that stood before Solomon his father while he yet lived, and said, How do ye advise that I may answer this people?

And they spake unto him, saying, If thou wilt be a servant unto this people this day, and wilt serve them, and answer

them, and speak good words to them, then they will be thy servants for ever.

But he forsook the counsel of the old men, which they had given him, and consulted with the young men that were grown up with him, and which stood before him:

And he said unto them, What counsel give ye that we may answer this people, who have spoken to me, saying, Make the yoke which thy father did put upon us lighter?

And the young men that were grown up with him spake unto him, saying, Thus shalt thou speak unto this people that spake unto thee, saying, Thy father made our yoke heavy, but make thou it lighter unto us; thus shalt thou say unto them, My little finger shall be thicker than my father's loins.

I Kings 12:4-10

After the death of King Solomon, the congregation of Israel came to Rehoboam, the son of Solomon, at Shechem. All of Israel actually came to Shechem to make him king. The first step taken by Rehoboam was a judicious one. No doubt he sought to cement the dissatisfied Ephraimites to himself by being crowned king in their chief city. This should have caused them to submit to the tribe of Judah, as this was a great honor afforded them, but their response was just the opposite.

Shechem lay on the flank of Mount Gerizim, directly opposite Mount Ebal, at the mount of curses and blessings (Deut 11:29, 27:1-8). It was a national sanctuary and the site of Abraham's first altar.

The congregation came complaining about the oppression of the people and hoping for certain changes in the attitude of the kings of the house of David. They agreed to continue being ruled by them if they would only lighten their burden.

Notice Rehoboam's reply: "Depart ye for three days, then come again to me." Rehoboam then consulted with the old men who had been with his father and had provided the Word of the Lord, the mind of God and the vision of God unto him. They gave him the right advice. They provided him with the Word of the Lord. They taught him how to hear God's Voice and flow with His leading.

They advised him with true counsel, saying he should be kind and lighten the burden for his subjects. But instead of obeying the counsel of God from the older men, the Bible says that Rehoboam decided to seek the counsel of the young men. We have believers in the Body of Christ that do likewise. We prefer advice from our buddies than from those who are familiar with the Presence of God. We become clogged and stubborn when God begins to counsel us through men upon whom He has placed His mantle. The end result of such a believer like Rehoboam is always disastrous. The Church has to hear from God! There are even many ministers whose churches and ministries are on the verge of collapse because of wrong counsel and advice from spiritually young men. I am talking about men that have not been trained accurately concerning how to hear, understand and flow with the leading of the Spirit. The Church needs the older men today, not just in age, but in the strength of the spirit. The Church needs men whose minds are clear, whose visions are real and whose ears can hear the prophetic sounds of revival and restoration.

CHAPTER II

THE DEVELOPMENT OF THE SPIRIT MAN

The development of our spirit man is very essential to our ability to understand God's guidance system. Our spirit can be educated and improved, just as our minds can be educated and improved. Man's spirit can be trained and built up just as the body can be built up.

> **But the natural man receiveth not the things of the Spirit of God: for they are foolishness unto him: neither can he know them, because they are spiritually discerned.**
>
> **I Corinthians 2:14**

Spiritual things cannot be understood with our natural mind. The mind must be changed. It must be renewed by God's power and Word in order for us to clearly understand and know when God speaks or is leading us in a certain direction. Man is a spirit. He has a soul and he lives in a body.

> **God is a Spirit: and they that worship him must worship him in spirit and in truth.**
>
> **John 4:24**

Jesus told the Samaritan woman, "God is a Spirit, and they that worship Him must worship Him in Spirit and in Truth." We cannot know God or touch Him physically. God is not a man. God is a Spirit. We cannot communicate with God and hear from God through our mental faculties. But, we can touch Him with our spirit. It is through our spirit that we can come to know God.

THE CREATIONAL PROCESS OF THE SPIRIT OF MAN

Let's see God's creation of the spirit part of man.

And God said, Let us make man in our image, after our likeness: and let them have dominion over the fish of the sea, and over the fowl of the air, and over the cattle, and over all the earth, and over every creeping thing that creepeth upon the earth.

Genesis 1:26

Every time God decides to create a thing, He operates according to three vital principles:

- First of all, He decides what He wants. The earth was void and there was nothing God could copy from in creating the world. He has to make or create original things.
- Secondly, He decides what He wants to make it out of or from.
- Thirdly, He speaks it forth or out of His mouth. God does nothing without first speaking it into existence.

Example:

And God said, Let the earth bring forth grass, the herb yielding seed, and the fruit tree yielding fruit after his kind, whose seed is in itself, upon the earth: and it was so.

And God said, Let there be lights in the firmament of the heaven to divide the day from the night; and let them be for signs, and for seasons, and for days, and years:

And God said, Let the waters bring forth abundantly the moving creature that hath life, and fowl that may fly above the earth in the open firmament of heaven.

And God said, Let us make man in our image, after our likeness: and let them have dominion over the fish of the sea, and over the fowl of the air, and over the cattle, and over all the earth, and over every creeping thing that creepeth upon the earth.

Genesis 1:11, 14, 20, 26

Verse 11: When God wanted grass and herbs in the earth, He spoke to the earth to produce it.

Verse 14: When God wanted light on the earth, He spoke to the firmament to produce the light. God did not speak to the earth or water to produce light. He instead spoke to the firmament.

Verse 20: And when God wanted to create the living creatures, He spoke to the water to produce them and not the earth.

Verse 25: But when God was to make man, it was very different. God could not make man out of the firmament, the earth or from the sea. Instead, God decided to make man from His own product.

MADE VERSUS CREATED

The words *MADE* and *MAKE* are used in the same context because they have the same meaning. The words MADE and MAKE are quite different from the word CREATE. The Hebrew word for MAKE or MADE is "ASAH," which means "to form out of something that is already there or already in existence." The word CREATE is derived from the Hebrew word "BAA." This means "to make from nothing." Since God could not make man out of the earth, firmament, water or the sea, God then decided to make man out of His own material.

What is this material? His image and likeness. The word IMAGE is derived from the Hebrew word "TSELEM" which means "shade, resemblance, figure of the Spirit." The word LIKENESS is derived from the Hebrew word "DEMOOTH," and it means MODEL, SHAPE and SIMILITUDE. God is a Spirit. All of His material is Spirit. So when man was made, man was made a spirit. Man is a spirit because of where man came from. When God made man, there was no gender. There were neither males nor females. Male and female was man. Since man is a spirit, made out of the product and material of God, man could not appreciate the earth because he was not made out of the earth. Man can only appreciate the Spirit because that is what he was made from. But man needs to appreciate the earth, because it is the earth that produces what man needs to survive in his earthly suit.

THE GENESIS PRINCIPLES

Let us consider some other principles here.

The first principle is that everything will appreciate a thing if they come from that thing. Man did not come from the earth, water, or firmament, so man cannot fully appreciate it. Man was only able to appreciate the Spirit because that is where he comes from. So in order for man to appreciate the earth, he needed to be made from or out of the earth. Without this, man would not appreciate and associate himself with the earth.

The second principle is that wherever a thing comes from, that thing must remain attached to that place for it to live or survive. Take these examples: fish need the water. The fish will appreciate the water more than the couch in your living room. The plant needs the soil to survive because it comes from the soil. The plant will appreciate the soil more than the stove in your kitchen. The stars needs the firmament to survive because that is where they come from. The stars will appreciate the firmament more than the water or the soil. The animals need the forest on the dry land to survive because that is where they come from. They will not appreciate your kitchen.

So also does man need God to survive, because man comes from God. Man is the product of God's Spirit. Man is supposed to appreciate God more than the water or the firmament. The day you leave your attachment is the day that you will die.

The third principle is that everything is made of the same components as its origin. God is love, because love comes from God. That means that we have the component of love in us. God is holy, because holiness comes from God. We have the component of holiness in us.

CREATION OF THE BODY

And every plant of the field before it was in the earth, and every herb of the field before it grew: for the LORD God had not caused it to rain upon the earth, and there was not a man to till the ground.

And the LORD God formed man of the dust of the ground, and breathed into his nostrils the breath of life; and man became a living soul.

Genesis 2:5, 7

Even though God said let us make man in our image and likeness in Genesis 1:26, we realize that the man created in Genesis 1:26 was the spirit man. God has no flesh or body into which He could make us. But because God is a Spirit, He created man in His image and likeness. That is the image and likeness of the Spirit (His Spirit). Genesis 2:5, 7 begins to tell us about the creation of man's flesh or body. The Bible tells us in the last line of Genesis 2:5, that there was not a man to till the ground. This is interesting. One might ask, why wasn't there a man to till the ground, when God actually made man in His image in Genesis 1:26?

The reason is that the man who was made in Genesis 1:26 was a man without body and flesh. He was a man made to resemble and in the figure of the Spirit. It was the spirit man. It is quite different from the man recorded or made in Genesis 2:5, 7.

And every plant of the field before it was in the earth, and every herb of the field before it grew: for the LORD God had not caused it to rain upon the earth, and there was not a man to till the ground.

And the LORD God formed man of the dust of the ground, and breathed into his nostrils the breath of life; and man became a living soul.

Genesis 2:5, 7

Let's see again the above Scripture carefully. Because man is a product of God's Spirit and because man had not yet been made from the earth, man did not appreciate the earth and man was not attached to the earth or the ground. So in order to make man a part of the earth, man had to have an earthly suit. As a result of this, God decided to make man out of the product of the earth called DUST.

> **Thus the heavens and the earth were finished, and all the host of them.**
>
> **And on the seventh day God ended his work which he had made; and he rested on the seventh day from all his work which he had made.**
>
> **And the LORD God formed man of the dust of the ground, and breathed into his nostrils the breath of life; and man became a living soul.**
>
> **Genesis 2:1-2, 7**

The word DUST comes from the Hebrew word "APHAR" which means MUD and RUBBISH. That means that God made man out of the same product from which He had made the grass and the herb. That product is the earth, which means "dry land full of rubbish (garbage)." God made man out of garbage. This allows man to appreciate the earth, thereby eating the things that the earth produces for his survival. Being made out of the earth– dust– entitled man to his earthly suit.

THE CREATION OF THE SOUL

> **And the LORD God formed man of the dust of the ground, and breathed into his nostrils the breath of life; and man became a living soul.**
>
> **Genesis 2:7**

When God first created man, He formed him out of the dust of the ground, and then breathed "the breath of life" into his nostrils. As soon as the breath of life, which became man's spirit, came into contact with man's body, the soul was produced. Therefore, the soul is the combination of man's body and spirit. The Scripture, therefore, called man a "living" soul. The breath of life became man's spirit; this is the principle of life within him.

The original meaning of the word LIFE in "breath of life" is "CAY" and is in the plural. This refers to the fact that the inbreathing of God produced a two-fold life: soulish and spiritual. When the inbreathing of God entered man's body, it became the spirit of man. But when the spirit reacted with the body, the soul was produced. This explains the source of our spiritual and soulish lives. "Formed man out of the dust of the ground," refers to man's body. "Breathed into his nostrils the breath of life," refers to man's spirit as it comes from God. And "man became a living soul," refers to man's soul when the body was quickened by the spirit and brought into being a living and self-conscious man.

According to Genesis 2:7, man was made up of only two independent elements, the corporeal and the spiritual. But when God placed the spirit within the casing of the earth, the soul was produced. "Man became a living soul" expresses not merely the fact that the combination of spirit and body produced the soul. In other words, soul and body were combined with the spirit, and spirit and body were merged in the soul.

God treated man's soul as something unique. As the angels were created as spirits, so also was man created predominately as a living soul. Man not only had a body– a body with the breath of life– but man became a living soul, as well. Man's soul represents him and expresses his individuality. It is the organ of man's free will; the organ in which spirit and soul are completely merged. If man's soul wills to obey God, it will allow the spirit to rule over the man as ordered by God. The soul, if it chooses, can also suppress the spirit and take some other delight as lord of the man.

The trinity of spirit, soul and body can be well illustrated with the help of a light bulb. Let's assume the bulb represents the total man. There is electricity, light and wires. The spirit is like the electricity; the soul is the light and the body is the wire. Electricity (spirit) is the cause of the light (soul) and light (soul) is the effect of the electricity (spirit). The wire (body) is the material substance for carrying the electricity (spirit) and also for manifesting the light (soul).

It must be planted in us, that man is a spirit being. He is made in the likeness of God. Jesus said that God is a Spirit (John 4:24). So man must, of necessity, be a spirit. Man has a soul and he lives in a physical body (Thess. 5:23).

MAINTENANCE OF MAN'S SPIRIT

Since we know that man is a spirit, that he has a soul and that he lives in a body, it would be valuable therefore to know and understand how to develop and maintain man's recreated human spirit, so that man can be able to effectively hear and understand when God is speaking and leading Him. Man's spirit can be maintained to a higher equivalency of how he was created in the following ways: by the renewal of the mind and by learning to meditate and feed on God's Word.

RENEWING OF THE MIND

I beseech you therefore, brethren, by the mercies of God, that ye present your bodies a living sacrifice, holy, acceptable unto God, which is your reasonable service.

And be not conformed to this world: but be ye transformed by the renewing of your mind, that ye may prove what is that good, and acceptable, and perfect, will of God.

Romans 12:1-2

The minds of the Body of Christ need cleansing. Our minds need to be renewed by the Word of God. For us to be able to hear, understand and interpret both the leading and Voice of God, we must have a renewed mind. Our minds must not be filled up with junk. A lot of Christians have problems understanding God's guidance system because of this predicament. Their minds are cluttered with the things of this world. It is not surprising that when God begins to speak to these individuals, they are unable to hear Him. We have a lot of believers that are distrustful and "leery-minded."

Paul begins to speak to us by beseeching us. The word "beseech" is a verb PARAKALEO. It comes from the prefix "para," which means "beside," and the suffix "kaleo," which means "call." So it literally means "call alongside." It was first used in the sense of "calling to one's side," or "to summon." The Berkeley and Weymouth translation used the words "beg and plead with." This is important to understand. Paul is literally begging and pleading with the Church to renew their minds. He knew the benefit of mind renewal and he also knew the danger of its neglect.

In this Scripture, there are some vital words that Paul used that must be considered in the light of what we are talking about in dealing with the renewal of the mind. Paul used the following important words: "present," "bodies," "reasonable service," "conformed," "world," "transformed" and "prove." These words are worth considering. The understanding of these words will actually shed more light on what Paul is saying to us today.

Paul pleaded with the Church to "present your bodies." He said, "that ye present." The word "present" means "to offer or to bring." It means "to make a decisive dedication once and for all." It means "to place your bodies at the disposal of God." We have a lot of believers who have not learned to place their bodies at the disposal of God. They want to hear what God is saying. They want to understand His leading and hear His Voice, yet they will not place their bodies at His disposal. We will need to make a once and for all decisive dedication. We must realize that, in order for us to be able to hear clearly the Voice of God concerning our lives, there must be a decisive dedication and a disposal of our body to God. The body must be crucified and put under subjection.

Mentioning of the "bodies" may be strange at first thought. There are a lot of us who take this literally as referring to the physical body. I like the way the Weymouth translation put it. It says, "all your faculties." It means "all of our whole being." All of our faculties need to be put at the disposal of God. Our body must be under the control of the Holy Spirit. All of our faculties and ways must be submitted to Him. This will cause the "real you" to come alive! When the "real you" comes alive, then understanding the leading and hearing the Voice of God becomes very easy.

Paul lets us know that this is our reasonable service. This is a service that is demanded by God of His people. "Reasonable service" means "the service of worship of God according to the requirement of the Levitical Law." It is the service which rationally corresponds to the moral premises contained in the faith which we professed and it is a worship with understanding. We must not think twice whether to present our bodies or not. We need not ponder whether it is right or wrong. We must put our full faculties at the disposal of God because it is the attitude, behavior and way which rationally corresponds to the promises contained in the Word of God.

Paul began to admonish us not to conform to this world. The man who conforms cannot be transformed. Men who conform cannot hear what God is saying. They can only hear what the devil and the world has to say. The term "AION" is translated "world" and "age" here in the King James Version. Basically, it means "a segment of time, an age." It is used of the present age, the age to come and also of eternity. The word "age" is the more usual meaning of the term "world" here in this Scripture. Paul encourages the Body of Christ to be transformed by the renewing of the mind. The mind must be transformed. It can only be transformed when it is renewed by the Word of God.

The word transform actually comes from a verb "METAMORPHOO." The word comes from "META" meaning "across" and "MORPHE" which means "form." So it means "to change across from one form to another." The biological expression "metamorphosis" comes from this word. This is a parallel account of the transfiguration (Matt. 17:2, Mark 9:2). In these Scriptures, it is rendered "transfigured." The usage of this word in the New Testament gives insight on how to live the transfigured life.

On the Mount of Transfiguration, the glory of Jesus burst through the veil of flesh and the disciples caught a glimpse of His eternal glory. Just as when we are transformed by the renewing of our mind, something of the divine glory within us will shine through our lives. Sandy and Healam thoroughly brought out the difference between the Greek words for "conform" and "transform" with this paraphrase: "Do not adopt the external and fleeting fashion of this world, but be ye transformed in your innermost nature."

Once this is done, the Bible tells us that we will be able to PROVE the good, acceptable and perfect will of God. The will of God is the Word of God. It is the mind of God. It is what God will tell you if you will accurately hear and understand His leading and His Voice. Paul says, "that ye may prove." The verb for the word PROVE is "DOKIMAZO." It means "to discover and to discern." It means "to make out." It means "to learn by experience" and it means "to find and follow." God wants us to be able to PROVE all things. When a believer's mind is transformed by the Word, he or she will be able to discover, discern and make out what God is saying. Understanding the guidance systems of God becomes very easy to you. Many believers have not been transformed by the Word of God and yet they want to PROVE what God is saying. That is impossible. It takes transformation of the Word to understand PROVING.

The Bible lets us know that once all these are completed, we will then be able to make out what the good, acceptable and perfect will of God is. A lot of Christians don't understand what this means. There are many believers today in the good will of God. They become complacent because the Bible says it is "good." They forget that there is an acceptable and a perfect will of God.

The word "good" here simply means "beneficial." That means that there is a beneficial will of God and the word "beneficial" means "something that contributes to a valuable end." The valuable has not been achieved, but the good will of God will just make a contribution that will enable that believer to reach the desired end, which is the perfect will. The "good" is the foundation and the take-off point toward the "perfect will" of God.

The "acceptable will," on the other hand, means "worthy, pleasing and welcome." This also contributes to the desired end. Although it is worthy, pleasing and welcome, it is still not the desired end.

Finally, the "perfect" means "complete, faultless and mature." This is God's desired end for His people. God wants His people to be complete and mature in every area so that they will be able to discern, discover and recognize His Presence. God wants His people to know, understand and be able to comprehend when He is leading. This is why we don't need to be relaxed and become complacent in the good and acceptable will of God. We must desire to come to that point in our Christian experience where we hear and speak to God without any hinderances. The Church must come to the point where she can tell when God is speaking and leading without any doubt. The Church must come to the place of accuracy and spiritual sharpness concerning the things of God. To do this, we must learn to renew our mind with the Word of God. There is no short cut to developing the ability to hear from God.

MEDITATING ON THE WORD

When believers today hear the word "meditation," they frequently associate it with a time consuming task, but what they actually fail to realize is that meditation adds a refreshing quality to the study of the Word. Meditation in the Word of God is one of the greatest keys to obtaining understanding through hearing the Voice of God. It is not surprising that the devil continually tries to destroy the message of meditation on God's Word.

Meditation means "to walk and talk and to memorize." It means to visualize and personalize the Word of God. It means to fill your thoughts with the thoughts of God and become consumed with the thoughts of God and the things which God has said. When this is done, it becomes very easy for a believer to understand and hear when God is speaking.

> **This book of the law shall not depart out of thy mouth; but thou shalt meditate therein day and night, that thou mayest observe to do according to all that is written therein: for then thou shalt make thy way prosperous, and then thou shalt have good success.**
>
> **Joshua 1:8**

This is a very powerful Scripture. God is saying, "If you will meditate on My Word day and night, and speak that Word and obey it, everything in your life will be prosperous and successful." One purpose of meditation is to position that believer in the place of doing God's Word. Another purpose of meditation is to position the believer in the right place where he or she can be able to know when God is speaking. Meditation in God's Word will also help the believer understand clearly the leading of the Lord.

Meditation will cause you to respond to God's Word with action. The results of meditating on the Word of God are tremendous!

> **This book of the law shall not depart out of thy mouth; but thou shalt meditate therein day and night, that thou mayest observe to do according to all that is written therein: for then thou shalt make thy way prosperous, and then thou shalt have good success.**
>
> **Have not I commanded thee? Be strong and of a good courage; be not afraid, neither be thou dismayed: for the LORD thy God is with thee whithersoever thou goest.**
>
> **Joshua 1:8-9**

Notice what the Scripture says. It says, "Thou shalt make thy way prosperous." That means *you!! You* are responsible for your own prosperity! It is determined by the extent and degree of your commitment towards meditating on God's Word. Remember, it is God's Word and not what the world says. It is only in the King James Version that the word "success" is written and recorded. When we begin to give ourselves completely to meditating on God's Word, God will then become the guarantee of our success and profit.

> **Blessed is the man that walketh not in the counsel of the ungodly, nor standeth in the way of sinners, nor sitteth in the seat of the scornful.**
>
> **But his delight is in the law of the LORD; and in his law doth he meditate day and night.**
>
> **And he shall be like a tree planted by the rivers of water, that bringeth forth his fruit in his season; his leaf also shall not wither; and whatsoever he doeth shall prosper.**
>
> **Psalms 1:1-3**

The man that walks in the counsel of the ungodly is the man that listens, receives, and accepts the advice of the enemy. There will be no blessing for such a man. But there will be blessings for the man who instead listens and accepts what God is saying and applies it to his life. In order for us to be in this position, we must learn to delight ourselves in the law (the Word of God) and meditate upon it day and night.

> **This book of the law shall not depart out of thy mouth; but thou shalt meditate therein day and night, that thou mayest observe to do according to all that is written therein: for then thou shalt make thy way prosperous, and then thou shalt have good success.**
>
> **Joshua 1:8**

In this text, "meditation" is divided into three parts:

- "This book of the law shall not depart out of thy mouth." This refers to the mouth.
- "But thou shalt meditate therein day and night." This refers to the act of meditation.
- "That thou mayest observe to do according to all that is written therein." This has to do with obeying and acting on God's Word.

These three parts actually birth the promise into your life. "For then thou shalt make thy way prosperous, and then thou shalt have good success."

It is impossible to read your Bible twenty-four hours a day without stopping. No one can continue reading his or her Bible twenty-four hours a day and expect to get anything else done. We must learn time management. We must learn how to arrange our time so that we can utilize the maximum potential of what has been allotted to us. Many believers are so busy that they find it difficult to set time aside in the morning, afternoon or evening to meet with God. He who does not meet with his Father daily will not know what the Father looks like.

We can afford to do everything else on our job and in the church, but when it comes to spending time with God, it becomes a problem. The funny thing about this is that we desire to know how to hear the Voice of God, and desire to experience prosperity and to be successful. God's price for meditation is high; there are no short cuts. Each believer must have special meditation time, starting first thing in the morning. Our mind is in its freshest and clearest position in the mornings. It is like a blackboard without any writing on it. It is uncluttered with cares or thoughts. When the Word of God is continually fresh in your spirit through meditation, it will protect you throughout the day and during the night.

WAYS OF MEDITATION

There are three biblical ways of meditation. They are as follows:

a) Learning to speak the Word aloud so that your ears can hear what you are saying. The Hebrew word for "speak" is the same as "to mediate." When you begin to tell believers and unbelievers about the great God we serve, about His power and His strength, we are actually meditating. Learn to talk about what God is doing. Whatever is in your heart will come out of your mouth in abundance. Do you know that anxiety and worrying is a form of meditation? The problem is that this is a wrong kind of meditation. When you begin to ponder and think and speak aloud about that negative situation in your life, what you are simply doing is meditating on the devil's junk!

b) The next way of meditating is by musing on God's Word. The word "muse" means "to ponder, think, consider and to carefully study a thing." This is common among most believers. This has to do with an individual taking a thought or a promise of God's Word and keeping it under their continual consideration. This has to do with memorization. Many believers get uptight as soon as the word "memorization" is mentioned. Some believers will say, "Listen, I am too old for that memorization stuff." They actually believe that memorization is meant for the younger Christian. This is why most ministers and believers are unable to quote a Scripture by heart. They cannot even tell you where the Scripture is found. This is very embarrassing and humiliating. The Church needs to meditate on the Word so much that the Word becomes a part of them.

c) Finally, I will consider the muttering of the soundness of God's Word.

> **This book of the law shall not depart out of thy mouth; but thou shalt meditate therein day and night, that thou mayest observe to do according to all that is written therein: for then thou shalt make thy way prosperous, and then thou shalt have good success.**
>
> **Joshua 1:8**

Joshua said, "This book of the law shall not depart out of thy mouth." This involves speaking of the Word out of your mouth. The only difference here is that the words are spoken quietly, as if one is speaking under his or her breath.

Muttering of the Word helps a lot. You can use it while in the laundry room. During your study of the Word, it is advisable to take two or three promises of God in His Word and begin to mutter them to yourself. It is very enriching and will thoroughly bless you.

We need meditation. We need to spend more time with God and meditate upon His Word. It will bring a great development to the spirit man and when this is accomplished, our minds will learn to be quiet long enough so that we can hear, understand and interpret the Voice and leading of God.

CHAPTER III

LEARNING SENSITIVITY

God is demanding and calling for sensitivity of heart. We must develop a sensitive heart in order to understand God's guidance system. To be sensitive, according to the New Webster's Dictionary, means to have the capacity and the ability to receive and perceive impressions from both internal and external influences. Sensitivity also refers to the readiness of nerves to respond to stimuli and the extent to which a radio device responds to incoming signals. We must develop the ability to receive and perceive impressions from the Presence of God. Our spiritual nerves and antenna must be highly developed and put in a state of readiness to respond to the stimuli and signal of the Holy Spirit.

And, behold, there cometh one of the rulers of the synagogue, Jairus by name; and when he saw him, he fell at his feet,

And besought him greatly, saying, My little daughter lieth at the point of death: I pray thee, come and lay thy hands on her, that she may be healed; and she shall live.

And Jesus went with him; and much people followed him, and thronged him.

And a certain woman, which had an issue of blood twelve years,

And had suffered many things of many physicians, and had spent all that she had, and was nothing bettered, but rather grew worse,

When she had heard of Jesus, came in the press behind, and touched his garment.

For she said, If I may touch but his clothes, I shall be whole.

And straightway the fountain of her blood was dried up; and she felt in her body that she was healed of that plague.

And Jesus, immediately knowing in himself that virtue had gone out of him, turned him about in the press, and said, Who touched my clothes?

And his disciples said unto him, Thou seest the multitude thronging thee, and sayest thou, Who touched me?

And he looked round about to see her that had done this thing.

But the woman fearing and trembling, knowing what was done in her, came and fell down before him, and told him all the truth.

And he said unto her, Daughter, thy faith hath made thee whole; go in peace, and be whole of thy plague.

Mark 5:22-34

This is a great example of one that possesses and operates in the spirit of sensitivity. Jairus, a ruler of the synagogue, came to Jesus begging for hands to be laid on his daughter who was at the point of death. Jesus, in responding to Jairus' request, was followed and thronged by a large crowd of people. Among the crowd was a woman with an issue of blood. Notice that she was in the crowd and that Jesus did not know that she was there.

But the Bible says that she said within herself, "If I may touch His clothes, I shall be whole." The woman only touched Jesus' garments. She did not touch Jesus's body. But because Jesus possessed the ability and a capacity to perceive impressions from both internal and external forces, He immediately knew that virtue had gone out of Him. Notice the word IMMEDIATELY. It did not take Him hours or days to know and tell if virtue had left Him or not. He knew immediately. This is beautiful! This is a great portrait of a sensitive Man! If it were one of us today, we might not even notice the difference. We might not be able to tell whether virtue has left from our being or not.

But because Jesus possessed and operated in sensitivity, His spiritual nerves were constantly in a state of readiness to respond to stimuli and incoming signals from the Presence of His Father. The Church must learn, develop and constantly operate in the spirit of sensitivity. We must develop sensitivity in these perilous times. It should not take us hours, days, weeks and months to detect if God is leading or not. We should be able to pick up on what is right or wrong immediately.

THE INSENSITIVE CHRISTIAN

> **Lo, he goeth by me, and I see him not: he passeth on also, but I perceive him not.**
>
> **Job 9:11**

Job begins here to paint for us the picture of a man or a woman that is not sensitive. The Bible says, "Lo, he goeth by me, and I see him not." We have a lot of believers with this same problem today. They are so insensitive to the things of God. Because of this insensitivity, they cannot perceive spiritual impressions from the Presence of God. They are unable to detect incoming signals. Their antennas are not in a state of readiness. Their spiritual nerves are dead. As we begin to develop the spirit of sensitivity, we will begin to perceive the Spirit of God every time He is in our midst.

STONY HEART

A new heart also will I give you, and a new spirit will I put within you: and I will take away the stony heart out of your flesh, and I will give you an heart of flesh.

And I will put my spirit within you, and cause you to walk in my statutes, and ye shall keep my judgments, and do them.

Ezekiel 36:26-27

Sensitivity cannot be operated in its full measure and intensity if our heart is stony. We must continually walk with the heart of flesh which was given to us when we were born-again. God has given us the heart of flesh and not of stone so that we may sense His Presence and His leading.

HOW TO DEVELOP SENSITIVITY OF HEART

In order for us to develop sensitivity, we must give the Word of God first place in our lives. You cannot be so busy neglecting your time of prayer, your time of fasting and the studying of the Word, and expect to operate in sensitivity. We must give quality time to the study of the Word. Notice what I said: study and not reading. There is a difference between studying and reading. Through studying, you become a spiritual investigator as to what God is saying. You diligently research and find meanings of words for clarity's sake. But in reading, you just rush through without really allowing the Spirit of God to highlight certain things to you. Your studying must be accompanied with meditation. Meditation brings reality to what you have studied. It allows the information in your head to sink down to your spirit. It is only from your spirit man that you can walk successfully as a believer.

We must give time to both personal and congregational prayer. We have believers in the Body of Christ that are so busy from Monday to Sunday that they never seem to have quality time to spend with the Lord. Most of them do their studying and praying on the train and bus while going to work or to other busy assignments. That is why most of us cannot perceive the Presence of God. That is why most believers cannot hear and understand when God is leading and speaking.

Game time is over! We must find time for the Word and prayer in our lives! We must determine to let go of some of those habitual and unnecessary assignments and allocate quality time to God! Don't you always notice in the Word that no matter how busy Jesus was, He always found quality time to spend with His Father? If Jesus could consistently do this, we can also do it, because He is our elder Brother, born of the same Daddy, God.

CHAPTER IV

LEARNING HOW TO RESPOND TO GOD'S VOICE AND LEADING

Often times it takes us hours, days, weeks, months and even sometimes years to respond to something God wanted us to do three weeks or two months ago. Many of us procrastinate concerning the Word of the Lord for our lives, ministries, church and family. God needs men and women who will be ready and willing to respond to His leading and Voice in His timing. It is very important to understand and learn how to respond to God when He speaks.

Even though briefly mentioned in the previous chapter, God wants us to develop a tender heart; that is, a heart that is succulent and free from any interruption of His leading. Unless our hearts are tender, spiritual things will be indistinct and unreal to us. When this happens, we will not be able to respond appropriately to the guiding of God. We will always be waiting, while He has actually spoken. Whatever channels or medium God chooses to use to speak to us, we must be prepared and ready to respond.

> **And he began again to teach by the sea side: and there was gathered unto him a great multitude, so that he entered into a ship, and sat in the sea; and the whole multitude was by the sea on the land.**
>
> **And he taught them many things by parables, and said unto them in his doctrine,**
>
> **Hearken; Behold, there went out a sower to sow:**
>
> **And it came to pass, as he sowed, some fell by the way side, and the fowls of the air came and devoured it up.**

And some fell on stony ground, where it had not much earth; and immediately it sprang up, because it had no depth of earth:

But when the sun was up, it was scorched; and because it had no root, it withered away.

And some fell among thorns, and the thorns grew up, and choked it, and it yielded no fruit.

And other fell on good ground, and did yield fruit that sprang up and increased; and brought forth, some thirty, and some sixty, and some an hundred.

And he said unto them, He that hath ears to hear, let him hear.

Mark 4:1-9

Some fell upon stony places, where they had not much earth: and forthwith they sprung up, because they had no deepness of earth:

And when the sun was up, they were scorched; and because they had no root, they withered away.

Matthew 13:5-6

When the Word of the Lord was released to the individual with the stony and hardened heart, the Bible says that "because it had no root, it withered away." In other words, the Word of the Lord did not produce any dividend because the heart that received it was stony, hardened and not pliable. The individual could not respond to the Word because he had no root or foundation upon which to build.

But other fell into good ground, and brought forth fruit, some an hundredfold, some sixtyfold, some thirtyfold.

Matthew 13:8

But in this verse of Scripture, the Bible begins to show us an example of an individual with a tender and succulent heart. The Bible says that the Word of the Lord "fell on good ground." In other words, the Word was received by men and women whose hearts were tender and as pliable as velvet. Notice here that they responded quickly to the Word. They received the Word of the Lord with joy and gladness. They did not procrastinate. The result of this was tremendous! They became fruitful! This is what God is calling for! Every one of us needs to learn how to respond appropriately and quickly to God's timing, Voice, leading and direction.

Two vital principles must be considered in learning how to respond to the Voice and leading of God.

- The Waiting Principle
- The Stillness Principle

THE WAITING PRINCIPLE

These wait all upon thee; that thou mayest give them their meat in due season.

Psalms 104:27

Lead me in thy truth, and teach me: for thou art the God of my salvation; on thee do I wait all the day.

Psalms 25:5

The LORD is good unto them that wait for him, to the soul that seeketh him.

Lamentation 3:25

We must learn to position ourselves in the place of waiting. Waiting has always been a problem with most believers. We find it difficult to wait. We cannot understand why we have to wait, especially those acquainted with the American culture where almost everything is quick, instant and rushed.

Food manufacturers produce food that will fortify the quick, instant and rushed mentality. Often, we bring these attitudes into Christendom. We always expect God to speak or lead us in two seconds or a minute, and when this is not done, we immediately give up and say in frustration, "God does not speak." The fact is, God still speaks. The problem is that the Church has not learned to position itself in the place of waiting so as to receive and respond to the Voice of God.

But they that wait upon the LORD shall renew their strength; they shall mount up with wings as eagles; they shall run, and not be weary; and they shall walk, and not faint.

Isaiah 40:31

"They that wait upon the Lord shall renew their strength." The word WAIT in Hebrew is "QARAH." It means "to expect, to bind together by twisting, or gather together and to look for with a view to a favorable reception." In other words, the Bible is saying that they that expect and look for with a view to a favorable reception will renew their strength. Notice that the waiting is for a favorable reception. From whom? From God!! The favorable reception brings the renewal of our strength. A person who craves for a favorable reception and does not know how to respond to this reception cannot experience the renewal of their strength.

We have to be properly positioned to look with great expectancy for a favorable reception from God and also be able to respond quickly when this reception comes. Notice the word "renew." The word "renew" in Hebrew is "CHAPLAH." This means "to change, to alter, to go forward, to grow up and to strike through." This is exactly what waiting does. This is what happens when we position ourselves in the place of waiting. Our lives begin to change from negative to positive. Our negative ways and attitudes begin to experience alterations into God's ways. We begin to move forward, grow up and strike through every barrier and impediment of the enemy.

> **... they shall mount up with wings as eagles; they shall run, and not be weary; and they shall walk, and not faint.**
>
> **Isaiah 40:31b**

Notice how the Bible likens us to the eagle. The eagle is one of the most powerful birds in the world. The eagle can mount to any altitude or level. "To mount" means "to climb, to rise, to go up and to ascend." God begins to liken the strength of the believer to the mounting power of the eagle. The Church represents God's eagles. As the Church begins to expect and look for with a view to a favorable reception from God, we will then begin to climb, rise and ascend in every endeavor. We will not be weary, weak or faint.

THE IMPORTANCE OF WAITING

Rest in the LORD, and wait patiently for him: fret not thyself because of him who prospereth in his way, because of the man who bringeth wicked devices to pass.

Psalms 37:7

Here we see the importance of waiting. The Bible says, "Rest in the Lord, and then wait patiently for Him." The word REST in Hebrew is "DOM." It means "to be silent, dumb and to calmly resign and leave all things in the Hand of God." This is a great lesson that we must learn. We must learn to resign from every situation and predicament that is coming our way and leave all things in the Hand of God. The Bible says for us to "rest," and then "wait."

Since we know the meaning of the word "wait," we then understand that we must first of all resign from every situation that the enemy has put or is trying to put upon us, and then look with a view to a favorable reception from God. This favorable reception brings the new and fresh direction from the leading of God.

THE STILLNESS PRINCIPLE

The stillness principle is also very essential to developing a responsive attitude to the Voice of God. You can be waiting and yet not be still at all. One is external and can be seen, and the other is internal and really cannot be seen. It takes the two principles working together for the believer to be effective in understanding God's guidance system. To "be still" means "to be fixed and firm." It means "to be silent, quiet, calm and serene, without agitation." Stillness is very essential to the reception of instructions.

And the LORD spake unto Moses, saying,

Speak unto the children of Israel, that they turn and encamp before Pihahiroth, between Migdol and the sea, over against Baalzephon: before it shall ye encamp by the sea.

For Pharaoh will say of the children of Israel, They are entangled in the land, the wilderness hath shut them in.

And I will harden Pharaoh's heart, that he shall follow after them; and I will be honoured upon Pharaoh, and upon all his host; that the Egyptians may know that I am the LORD. And they did so.

And the LORD hardened the heart of Pharaoh king of Egypt, and he pursued after the children of Israel: and the children of Israel went out with an high hand.

And when Pharaoh drew nigh, the children of Israel lifted up their eyes, and, behold, the Egyptians marched after them; and they were sore afraid: and the children of Israel cried out unto the LORD.

And they said unto Moses, Because there were no graves in Egypt, hast thou taken us away to die in the wilderness? wherefore hast thou dealt thus with us, to carry us forth out of Egypt?

And Moses said unto the people, Fear ye not, stand still, and see the salvation of the LORD, which he will show to you to day: for the Egyptians whom ye have seen to day, ye shall see them again no more for ever.

Exodus 14:1-4, 8, 10-11, 13

Here we see the stillness principle and its operation. The children of Israel, while leaving Egypt, had a "Red Sea" experience. God hardened the heart of Pharaoh and caused him to pursue the Israelites. The Bible lets us know that the Israelites became afraid and began to murmur and grumble against their leader, Moses. They said, "Is not this the word that we did tell thee in Egypt, saying, Let us alone, that we may serve the Egyptians?" I want you to notice carefully Moses' reply. Moses told the people to "fear not" and to "be still." Moses knew that in order to hear and understand the Voice and leading of God concerning the Red Sea, he had to be quiet, calm, firm and fixed upon God without any agitation.

We must learn this. Likewise, we must learn to be quiet, calm and fixed, without panicking or worrying in whatever situation the enemy might bring across our path. This is the only way that we can be able to effectively discern, hear and respond to the leading of God quickly. For us to experience the salvation, preservation, healing, wholeness, soundness and prosperity or the favor of the Lord in our lives, we must learn to operate in the stillness principle. The stillness principle is the passage that brings clarity and new directions.

> **And there were certain men, who were defiled by the dead body of a man, that they could not keep the passover on that day: and they came before Moses and before Aaron on that day:**
>
> **And those men said unto him, We are defiled by the dead body of a man: wherefore are we kept back, that we may not offer an offering of the LORD in his appointed season among the children of Israel?**
>
> **And Moses said unto them, Stand still, and I will hear what the LORD will command concerning you.**
>
> **Numbers 9:6-8**

The Scripture again brings clarity to the stillness principle. The children of Israel, while in the wilderness, were instructed and commanded by God through Moses to keep the

Passover feast. Although this was done, the Bible tells us that there were certain men who could not keep the Passover because they were "defiled by the dead body of a man."

See what the men did. They came before Moses and Aaron and told them why they were not participating in the feast. Look carefully at what Moses said. He said, "Stand still, and I will hear what the Lord will command concerning you." This is powerful. Moses refused to decide the fate of the men. He refused to okay their plea without first consulting God. Moses wanted to know God's mind concerning the situation. He wanted to be sure that whatever he said was from God. This is a reminder to the Church today. We must learn to consult God concerning every issue of life. Notice the words Moses used, "Stand still."

Moses was telling the men to be quiet, calm and remain fixed because he wanted to hear what the Lord had to say. Moses knew that stillness would bring clarity to God's Voice. When we begin to learn to be still in our situation, whether bad or good, we will begin to produce accurate and sharp men and women who will unfailingly move in the wisdom of God.

And as they were going down to the end of the city, Samuel said to Saul, Bid the servant pass on before us, (and he passed on,) but stand thou still a while, that I may show thee the word of God.

I Samuel 9:27

Be still, and know that I am God: I will be exalted among the heathen, I will be exalted in the earth.

Psalm 46:10

Also, Saul, in looking for his father's asses, was divinely connected with the prophet Samuel. God already spoke to Samuel concerning the choice of Saul as the king of Israel. Samuel feasted with Saul, and afterward he decided to send him away. The Bible says that as they were going down to the end of the city, Samuel told Saul to tell his servant to "pass on before us." But to Saul, he told him to "stand still for a while, that I may show thee the Word of the Lord." In order for the Word of the Lord to be given, Samuel and Saul had to be still. They had to be quiet, serene, calm and fixed. It is important to understand why stillness is needed before the Word is given. Stillness brings clarity. It brings understanding, comprehension and enables the interpretation of the Word of the Lord.

CHAPTER V

DEVELOPING THE SPIRIT OF DISCERNMENT FOR GUIDANCE

God guides His people. He does not leave you in confusion or frustration. Paul said God is not the author of confusion, but of peace and of order. So when people say "I am so confused," that is not God. God did not produce that. There is something wrong and it is in their ability to develop a strong spirit of discernment so as to understand God's guidance systems. God has navigating systems that He uses by His Spirit to guide us through life, so that we won't make major mistakes and walk in error. In order for us to properly embrace His navigational system, we must possess and walk in strong discernment. Discernment is that which is developed in the character of an individual more than through the subjective Holy Spirit insight that is usually defined with this word discernment as the gift of the Spirit. I personally believe, after being in the ministry now for a number of years, that discernment is in high order. Discernment is one of the virtues that we wish– no, more than wish– that we pray many more people will develop in their own lives.

Discernment is that part of Christian living which allows a person to make right decisions. Right decisions have ramifications. When you make a right decision, it causes right things to happen. It causes right feelings. It creates right guidance. It causes circumstances to line up. Right decisions are a marvelous part of life.

Wrong decisions are a terrible part of life. There is nothing worse than a wrong decision that you cannot undo quickly. Most wrong decisions are of that sort. There are decisions that we make financially, morally, socially, philosophically and conceptually. When we make a decision that is really wrong, we begin to pay for it. First emotionally and then spiritually, inside. That which is internal soon becomes external and we pay for it in our lifestyle. We pay for it in our circumstances. We pay for it even in our children. Wrong decisions are a terrible part of life. Now, I would like to say that I have always made right decisions, but that would be wrong. I have not always made right decisions. I have made some poor decisions, some definitely wrong decisions, and some grey decisions. But as you grow older in the Lord, hopefully, you protect yourself more and more, and make the kind of decisions that are basically in harmony with the wisdom of God. As that harmony begins to get worked out in your mind and in your lifestyle, it begins the work of peace, joy, stability, happiness and safety. It begins to work something anew that no one can take away. It is yours for life.

> **Of whom we have many things to say, and hard to be uttered, seeing ye are dull of hearing.**
>
> **For when for the time ye ought to be teachers, ye have need that one teach you again which be the first principles of the oracles of God; and are become such as have need of milk, and not of strong meat.**
>
> **For every one that useth milk is unskilful in the word of righteousness: for he is a babe.**
>
> **But strong meat belongeth to them that are of full age, even those who by reason of use have their senses exercised to discern both good and evil.**
>
> **Hebrews 5:11-14**

One of the five Hebrew words used for discernment has to do with hearing. Without the ability to hear from God, you do not have the capacity to develop discernment. Hearing and discernment go together. "You have become dull of hearing," the apostle said. "Though by this time you ought to be teachers, you have need again for someone to teach you the elementary principles." That is, "the beginning parts" or the "basics of the oracle." One of the Hebrew words for discernment is the word "to speak" and the word "oracle" means "the speaking place." You have need for someone to teach you again the oracles, that is, the Voice of God.

> **For every one that useth milk is unskilful in the word of righteousness: for he is a babe.**
>
> **Hebrews 5:13**

According to the Greek, the "word of righteousness" should be worded "the word of principles," or "the word that is established by principles." A mature person knows the Word that is established by the principles of God, the principles of His own spoken Word. Once you understand the principles of God, it is like a railroad track. You can put your car on it and you can go straight to the town you should be headed for, because you have a track to run on. It is called principle. Paul says those who are carnal, who only love milk and not principle, or to put it another way, those who love sensational spiritual activities more than the disciplines of the Christian life, are those who never grow up. Growing up and discernment are the same. The reason a child does not have perspective is because the child doesn't have discernment. It is because he is a child. He thinks like a child. He acts like a child. He eats like a child. He burps like a child. Paul is simply saying that those who are grown up are still acting like children. They are of age, but they are not of age. It is the idea of principles.

Solid food is for the mature who, because of practice, have their senses trained to discern good and evil. So discernment is something that comes through a discipline. It comes through the disciplines of developing the character of God and many other things. Out of that discipline comes a discernment wherein you understand what is inherently good and what is inherently evil, and how to eat of the tree of good and not to eat of the tree of evil. If someone says to you to do this, you immediately say, "That is the tree of evil. I am not eating from that tree."

> **Give therefore thy servant an understanding heart to judge thy people, that I may discern between good and bad: for who is able to judge this thy so great a people?**
>
> **I Kings 3:9**

Notice in I Kings 3:9, Solomon puts discernment on top of an understanding heart. Discernment and an understanding heart grow together. Discernment is something that is given along with the heart. There are some hints of where discernment comes from. Proverbs 2:6 says "For the Lord gives wisdom. From His mouth comes knowledge and discernment." Proverbs 5:2 says "That you may observe discretion and your lips may reserve knowledge ... that you may observe discernment."

PRINCIPLES TO DEVELOPING STRONG DISCERNMENT

There are five basic steps taken from the Hebrew words on how to develop discernment.

NAKAR

The first Hebrew word is "NAKAR" which means "to inspect or look something over with the intention of recognizing it, discerning it, and distinguishing between the good and evil parts of it." The word NAKAR speaks of the discipline of inspecting something before buying it. It is what the Israelites used to do before they went to get the oxen that they were going to use for their field. They didn't want to buy an ox that had a bad leg, a bad head or whatever. So they would inspect the ox or the animal.

It is the same word used for the priest. Before he would offer the sacrifice to God, he would inspect the sacrifice to make sure it was worthy to be offered. This word NAKAR carries the idea of detail, meticulous looking into something. Discernment has to do with the discipline of patience, looking at something long enough to see what it is really like. Inspect it. Look it over with the intention of discerning it and distinguishing its parts.

As a local church pastor I hear most singles ask why the need for premarital counseling. Then after they are married they say, "We wish more people would go through premarital counseling, because the woman or the man you end up with after the wedding day is sometimes not the same person you dated." Love is not only blind, it is also deaf and dumb. God gives us an emotional love toward each other. That is how He gets us together to get married, so that we can work on each other. Yet when I say to people, "Inspect your partner" they sometimes get upset. They swell up, get angry and red in the face. They say, "Who gives you the right to ask us all these questions? All we want to do is just get married!" After the wedding is over, and after a few months have passed, then they come back crying the blues and saying, "Pastor, we are not meant for each other. I had no idea this turkey was $5,000 in debt. Now I have to work and he is taking my money to pay his bills. All he is doing with his money is just buying clothes." You have to inspect before marriage.

The very first word in the Bible for discernment is one of the strongest words in the Bible for detail. Inspect the sacrifice. If the priest offered a sacrifice he did not inspect, and that sacrifice was blemished, God would kill the priest. He inspected it *slowly*. And before they offered it, the priest said, "Just one more time." Not only did they have to inspect the outward, they had to cut the animal open. There could be no inside bruises. Not just the outside, but the inside of the animal had to be without blemish, because it had to speak of the Lord Jesus Christ, Who was not only externally sinless, but internally sinless. Discernment is inspection, to look something over with the intention of discerning and recognizing it.

SHAMA

The second Hebrew word is "SHAMA." It means "to listen with the idea of obeying what you hear." The word SHAMA is the idea that when you hear something, you will gain perception. Effective hearing involves perception. The idea of understanding comes from perception, and perception comes from effective hearing, and effective hearing comes from expecting someone to talk to you. SHAMA is the idea of listening, hearing, gaining perception, obeying what you hear and gaining understanding so that you have discernment.

RAAI

The third Hebrew word is "RAAI." It means watching something and learning from it; that is, a video, listening to a tape, a preacher, a person in action or a circumstance, and learning from it. The idea here is that you watch something and you learn from it. I would much rather learn from someone else's pain than by doing it all on my own. I mean, if you want to hurt for me and model it for me, I would rather see you hurt, go through problems and learn from it, than to go through it myself. Doesn't that sound terrible? But that is wisdom. Wisdom is knowing that you don't have to feel every pain and go through every experience in life in order to have wisdom. The wisdom is in learning by watching. That is usually why the number one child has the hardest time. By the time you get down to child number three or four, he's learned from number one, two and three not to do certain things.

TEBUNA

The fourth Hebrew word is "TEBUNA." It means "the process whereby one gains knowledge through experience, and then through experience, gains discernment." What comes out of the word TEBUNA is the power of judgment or, as it is translated, "insight and discretion." It is not just gathering data. It is gathering life experiences and gaining perception and discretion.

YADA

The final Hebrew word is "YADA." YADA means a knowledge gained by your experiences, whether beneficial or harmful. Never, never focus on the people who offend you, because you will become like them. That is why Jesus talked so much of forgiveness, because He is saying don't focus. Don't let your emotions get attached. Don't let your whole life focus on that person or that thing or that circumstance, because you will become bitter, angry, or you will become the way that father or mother or aunt or friend or spouse was. Whatever you focus on, you will become. Therefore, forgive. Take your focus off them. Put your focus back on God and become like Him, not like them.

At some point in life you have to look at your experiences and determine whether those experiences shaped you into some kind of a monster. Will you forgive no matter what happened to you and focus on a loving God? Will you focus on God, become like Him, and let experiences have their place? When that happens, there is an amazing freedom. The next time you see that father or that mother or that spouse that has just been the most terrible person to you, and has caused you untold pain, you are not focusing on them with bitterness and hatred, but instead it's "Praise God!" You have freedom. A person that understands forgiveness will never allow negative focus to shape their life. According to the flesh, you should never forgive. You should get back at them. There should be vengeance in your blood. But according to the laws of God and discernment, you let go of the bad and you take in the good. You learn and you develop into a mature Christian.

CHAPTER VI

GOD'S CHANNEL OF COMMUNICATION

Love not the world, neither the things that are in the world. If any man love the world, the love of the Father is not in him.

For all that is in the world, the lust of the flesh, and the lust of the eyes, and the pride of life, is not of the Father, but is of the world.

And the world passeth away, and the lust thereof: but he that doeth the will of God abideth for ever.

But ye have an unction from the Holy One, and ye know all things.

I have not written unto you because ye know not the truth, but because ye know it, and that no lie is of the truth.

Let that therefore abide in you, which ye have heard from the beginning. If that which ye have heard from the beginning shall remain in you, ye also shall continue in the Son, and in the Father.

And this is the promise that he hath promised us, even eternal life.

These things have I written unto you concerning them that seduce you.

But the anointing which ye have received of him abideth in you, and ye need not that any man teach you: but as the same anointing teacheth you of all things, and is truth, and is no lie, and even as it hath taught you, ye shall abide in him.

I John 2:15-17, 20-21, 24-27

In studying the epistle of John, we find he was a man that was very concerned about spiritual development. John was interested in bringing the Body of Christ to spiritual maturity. He writes to children and to adults. This is a man to whom God has revealed a chartered plan to spiritual maturity. He possessed a blueprint for corporate understanding and growth in the Kingdom of God.

The most significant thing that the apostle John did was to bring the believer, the New Covenant men and women, into contact with the Holy Spirit. As a New Covenant believer, the issue is not whether God is speaking. The Scripture implicitly declares that God desires to speak to us. But the issue is over the methods of communication that God uses. How does God communicate? God wants to interact with us on a daily basis through the Holy Spirit. And He desires to lead us and to instruct us and there is not one simple area of our lives in which He is not interested. But the real issue is, how does God speak to us? How can I come in contact with Him and learn to hear and discern and to understand His Voice on a daily basis? As long as the devil can blind our eyes to that aspect of relationship or to the methods of communication that God uses, then he has us exactly where he wants us, because we will never clearly hear what the Holy Spirit is saying.

If Jesus said, "My sheep know My Voice," and if John said, "You have an anointing from the Holy One and know all things and that same anointing which abides within you produces the ability to teach you," then evidently there is an access vehicle of communication that God wants to use. Evidently, there is a sure way to identify the Voice of God when He is speaking to you. Christians often ask, "When I listen to God, how do I know that it is God? How do I know that it is not a false spirit or a familiar voice or a satanic influence?" Or, "When I listen to God, how do I know that I'm not hearing my own feelings? When God speaks to me, how do I know which voice is the right voice because I often hear two voices?"

Identifying the Voice of God is very essential to having confidence in what God is saying and doing. In order to have confidence in what is being said, you must first of all be able to identify the voice of the one that is talking. With knowledge comes confidence. With understanding comes the ability to lock your faith in and to follow thereafter. Until you understand the Guide, you will never understand the directions in which He is leading you. Consequently, your life is going to be filled with a series of questions like, "Why this?" and "Why that?"

It is important that we know that truth is not independent of thought. Truth is not a feeling. It is not a theory. It is not an attitude and it is not a perception. Truth is not a variable. Truth is a constant. Opinions are variable and perceptions are variable. Truth is a constant. Truth is unwavering and Truth is a Person. Everything that God says must be in harmony and in conjunction with His Word and must not contradict His thought.

The reason why God gave us the written Scripture and the reason why God speaks beyond the Scripture, is because you will encounter situations in your life that are not covered by Scriptures. If you seek to please God and to honor Him and be found faithful with that which God has given you, you will find yourself at a point presented with situations and circumstances in which the Word of God does not give a clear definition. For example, the Bible does not tell you where to live, whether in Africa, in Asia, in Russia or in Mexico. The Word of God does not give explicit instructions for each one of us to let us know our assigned geographical location.

But the Holy Spirit has something to say about where you should live. He desires to lead you into the green pastures that have been allotted for you. The Word of God also did not say whether you should marry Peter, Paul or Michael. The Word of God did not indicate the name of the person you should marry. Yet, the Holy Spirit desires to be intricately involved in bringing you together with your mate for life. The Word of God did not specifically tell you how many children you should bear. If you have the strength, the support and finances to have one, three or twenty, that is your responsibility. Yet, the Holy Spirit wants to be involved in the bringing forth of your family and show you how big your family should be. So these are ways in which the Scriptures are limited in their ability to bring specific guidance to our lives. But, the Holy Spirit is available to lead you, to guide you and to instruct you in every area of endeavor and decision.

The Bible did not say whether a Lexus is better than a Mercedes Benz or if a Volvo is better than a Cadillac, but the Holy Spirit is available to lead you into making the right choice for you. God wants to speak to you on a daily basis. While the Word of God is not clear in all of these areas, there are certain principles which support that these decisions are eternal. If you can learn these principles, then you can learn the attitudes of God, the heart of God and how He feels about certain situations.

And I will pray the Father, and he shall give you another Comforter, that he may abide with you for ever;

John 14:16

Jesus called the Holy Spirit "another Comforter. " Jesus was the first Comforter. The Holy Spirit was the second Comforter. He is One that is called alongside to help. One who will complete the initiative of the first Comforter. As a Comforter, called alongside to help, He will lead us and guide us. Now, let's look and examine some of the ways God speaks to us.

OUR RECREATED HUMAN SPIRIT

At times, many of God's people find it difficult to hear the Voice of God through their recreated human spirit. This is important, because God is still speaking to His people today through their recreated human spirit. Our recreated human spirit has two guides: the inward witness and the inward voice. The inward witness is different from the inward voice.

The inward witness is something inside of you that produces a check, a red light instructing you to stop. It is not a voice. It is an inward intuition. It is an inward knowing. It is a feeling that is produced in our spirit and not in our mind or body. If the Body of Christ learns and continues to follow the leadings that are produced from our inward witness, the Church will see and receive great guidance in every area of life. We would be able to avoid certain pitfalls that the enemy has placed in our path. The inward witness produces a burden for a thing. The word "burden" actually means "creating a sense of responsibility."

For thou wilt save the afflicted people; but wilt bring down high looks.

For thou wilt light my candle: the LORD my God will enlighten my darkness.

Psalms 18:27-28

Here, God lights our lamp. The Bible says that "The spirit of man is the candle of the Lord...." That means that our spirit is a lamp. It is a light. It guides and directs us. What then happens in the leading from the inward witness, is that God lights our spirit (which is the lamp), and allows us to see all of the tricks, schemes and devices of the enemy that lurk in the darkness. God allows us to avoid pitfalls by lighting our lamps. When the light goes on in us, we immediately have this knowing– this intuition– and are able to see the right path and make the right decisions.

The problem is, many of us do not follow the inward witness. We go in our own directions and make our own decisions. The inward witness demands faith, trust and complete reliance upon the leading of God. Many say to themselves, "What if God is not actually leading me?" The problem is that the spirit man has not been properly trained. We must respond to the inward witness by faith, knowing that God is actually speaking and leading.

But as it is written, Eye hath not seen, nor ear heard, neither have entered into the heart of man, the things which God hath prepared for them that love him.

But God hath revealed them unto us by his Spirit: for the Spirit searcheth all things, yea, the deep things of God.

For what man knoweth the things of a man, save the spirit of man which is in him? even so the things of God knoweth no man, but the Spirit of God.

But the natural man receiveth not the things of the Spirit of God: for they are foolishness unto him: neither can he know them, because they are spiritually discerned.

But he that is spiritual judgeth all things, yet he himself is judged of no man.

I Corinthians 2:9-11,14-15

The Spirit itself beareth witness with our spirit, that we are the children of God:

Romans 8:16

The spirit of man is the candle of the LORD, searching all the inward parts of the belly.

Proverbs 20:27

The Holy Spirit desires to invade us. Let me put it this way: He wants to light our lamps. You may have a dead candle. You may be dead in your trespasses and dead in your sins, but the Holy Spirit Himself will come and bear witness to your spirit that you are a child of God through the new birth process. He will strike the match and light your lamp. He will bring spiritual enlightenment because He sets up residence within you, as His headquarters, within your spirit man. The Holy Spirit headquarters in our spirit. Our spirit becomes His communication center. He then begins to communicate to us by speaking to our spirit through the inward witness– words, thoughts, feelings– that you know are not of yourself, but they are somehow within you.

The Holy Spirit will communicate through feelings. That is part of perceiving in the Spirit. This is why, when you have done certain things, you may feel a great feeling within your spirit man of peace and joy. You find that the Holy Spirit is pleased and He is communicating peace and joy. There are other times when things are wrong and the Holy Spirit is displeased and He communicates within you a grieving or a sorrow. The Holy Spirit can warn you by communicating with you through a tightness in your gut. Now, we are not talking about natural feelings. The Holy Spirit can communicate to you through promptings, leadings, and perceivings that may not be outright words, but they are inner knowings.

> **And when Simon saw that through laying on of the apostles' hands the Holy Ghost was given, he offered them money,**
>
> **Saying, Give me also this power, that on whomsoever I lay hands, he may receive the Holy Ghost.**
>
> **But Peter said unto him, Thy money perish with thee, because thou hast thought that the gift of God may be purchased with money.**
>
> **Thou hast neither part nor lot in this matter: for thy heart is not right in the sight of God.**
>
> **Repent therefore of this thy wickedness, and pray God, if perhaps the thought of thine heart may be forgiven thee.**
>
> **For I perceive that thou art in the gall of bitterness, and in the bond of iniquity.**
>
> **Acts 8:18-23**

There are times that you just know. How? Through spiritual perception. The spirit of a man goes out before the man. That is why people with the same spirit will usually find each other. People that have homosexual spirits have a very powerful demonic way of finding one another. That is the counterfeit to the genuine knowing of people by the spirit. That is why immorality will join with one another. That is why there is usually more unity in rebellion than there is in righteousness. Although it should not be this way, it usually is. Those in rebellion usually can attract to themselves others with the same rebellious spirit. From the above Scripture, you find that Paul was able to perceive that Simon was in the gall of bitterness.

THE INWARD VOICE

The inward voice is the voice of the conscience. It is the voice that echoes out of our conscience. Everybody has a conscience, whether a believer or an unbeliever. It is like a buzzer that sounds inside of us. With our conscience, we can tell if God is leading and speaking to us or not. When God begins to speak to you and you disobey Him, you can feel your conscience hurting. A lot of us might wonder if our conscience can actually be dependable. Our conscience can always be dependable, if our spirit man has become new.

> **I say the truth in Christ, I lie not, my conscience also bearing me witness in the Holy Ghost,**
>
> **Romans 9:1**

Look at what Paul was saying in Romans 9:1. He said he was not lying, and the reason he knew this was because his conscience was being enlightened and prompted by the Holy Spirit.

And Paul, earnestly beholding the council, said, Men and brethren, I have lived in all good conscience before God until this day.

Acts 23:1

In Acts 23:1, Paul began to tell the Sanhedrin that he has lived and walked before God performing all of his duty with a good conscience. Why? Because his conscience was constantly being enlightened and prompted by the Holy Spirit.

The steps of a good man are ordered by the LORD: and he delighteth in his way.

Psalms 37:23

What does this word "order" mean? If I am going to be ordered by the Lord in my directive of going out and coming in, then what does it mean to be "ordered?" Here we see David using the Hebrew word, which means "to be erect" or "to stand perpendicular."

What this therefore means is that the steps of a good man are erected or standing perpendicular by the Lord. The Hebrew word also contains another element of thought. It means to be directed, established, and led. It implies more than just direction. It includes divine appointment, prosperity and everything that pertains to the covenant promise of God. All this is contained in the word "order." Therefore we can say that the steps of a good man are established, directed, prospered, blessed, divinely appointed, and are established with strength and ability to stand perpendicular. It is all contained in being led by the Spirit. Being led by the Spirit is being established in the will of God. It is being directed by the Spirit of God and prospering in the Word of God. This must become a lifestyle to us.

If ye be willing and obedient, ye shall eat the good of the land:

Isaiah 1:19

Hearing the Voice of God is not what we do in a crisis. But it is a complete lifestyle that is sanctioned by obedience. When I obey God's Word for my life, I am opening the door for a consistent flow of communication with my Father. If you have a problem hearing the Voice of God, the first question you must ask yourself is whether or not you are obeying what the Word of God says to do. Are you doing what God has set forth clearly in the Word of God for you to do? If you are not good in obeying the Word of God, you will never be sensitive in hearing the Voice of God. It is a lifestyle of obedience.

Being led of the Holy Spirit often involves the introduction of God's ordained circumstances into our lives. Often, God will introduce circumstances into our lives to gain our attention. There are circumstances that are of God and there are circumstances that are not of God. If we don't know how to differentiate between what is of God and what is not of God, we will find ourselves following the wrong thing.

Woe unto them that call evil good, and good evil; that put darkness for light, and light for darkness; that put bitter for sweet, and sweet for bitter!

Isaiah 5:20

There is a definite, distinguishable line between God-ordained circumstances for our growth and development, and the circumstances that the devil introduces into our lives to sidetrack us. Circumstances alone cannot be taken as a reliable guide for the will of God in your life.

However, circumstances will be introduced, and they must be supported by two things. First, what does the Word of God have to say about these circumstances? God introduces circumstances in our lives for refinement, but these circumstances never contradict His established Word. Second, the measuring stick must be the witness of the Holy Spirit.

You see, we have a strange charismatic philosophy that temptations, testings and trials are only introduced when we miss God or when we sin. And when the enemy begins to challenge and buffet us, the first thing that we always do is ask God if there is any sin in our lives. Even though this is right, we must not camp there. We must be ready to move further. But a great deal of us are wrestling because we think that we have missed God or have sinned. We literally think that we are the elite crowd and that we are not susceptible to the contrary winds that must blow into each of our lives. There is no favoritism in the Kingdom of God, and God is not a respecter of persons.

When you find yourself in temptation and trials, you must know that they have come for your spiritual refinement.

> **Behold, I will send my messenger, and he shall prepare the way before me: and the Lord, whom ye seek, shall suddenly come to his temple, even the messenger of the covenant, whom ye delight in: behold, he shall come, saith the LORD of hosts.**
>
> **But who may abide the day of his coming? and who shall stand when he appeareth? for he is like a refiner's fire, and like fullers' soap:**
>
> **Malachi 3:1-2**

God is forever sitting as a Refiner. He is going to begin with the sons of Levi, because judgment first begins with the House of the Lord. It is going to begin with the priesthood. We sit around looking at ministers and watch them fall. We see them being purged and judged and we get the wrong idea that their circumstance is the location of the heat. That is partly true. The heat is going to come upon all of the Body of Christ generally, before God begins to wrap up His Church. And where we have sat criticizing, mocking and scorning in self-righteous attitudes, God is going to come upon every believer and He is going to purge us of our judgmentalism, our critical spirits, our mockery and the shameful lack of discipline that stains our tongues. It begins with the sons of Levi. But it will continue to the other members in the Body. The process of refinement is never easy, but it is vital to your spiritual development.

THE CONFIRMATION OF WITNESSES

God was very faithful to Old Testament Israel with a cloud in the day and a pillar of fire by night. He was meticulous in how He protected them and how He guided them. Today, there are unnecessary hurts, loss of revenues, broken relationships, terrible mistakes and tragedies in life because people simply do not know how God directs. People who often trust only one way of guidance usually want their own way. They know that if they go and get counsel, or if they go and examine that direction with the other ways God directs, they know that the answer will be no. So they say, I am trusting those three phone call confirmations. They end up losing.

This is the third time I am coming to you. In the mouth of two or three witnesses shall every word be established.

II Corinthians 13:1

Here is the key to God's navigation system. God is saying here that He will not allow us to be led by just one principle. There is too much danger. I am not saying at any time one is not right, but I am saying that, to make a major decision in your life, God will not allow you to be led by just one. The rule is, two or three at a minimum.

After they were come to Mysia, they assayed to go into Bithynia: but the Spirit suffered them not.

Acts 16:7

Then the Spirit said unto Philip, Go near, and join thyself to this chariot.

Acts 8:29

Several years ago, the cargo door of a Boeing 707 from Hawaii blew out and caused structural damage up above to the seating section. A number of the passengers were blown out into the Pacific Ocean and were killed. What was not in the news was that there was a Spirit-filled Christian who was sitting right next to where the accident occurred who gave a testimony and said that just moments before the disaster, he heard a Voice in his spirit saying he should move to another area of the plane. He hesitated a moment and the Voice said move now. He did not hear it audibly. He heard it in his spirit. So he got up and moved to an unoccupied seat in the coach area and moments later the section where he had been sitting was ripped out. Now that is the ability to be led by an inner conviction, the small Voice of the Holy Spirit which gives you a thought, a picture or an impression inside. This is exactly what Paul experienced. He and the men were on their way to their intended assignment. But they were stopped by the Spirit. They were stopped by this inner conviction or this impression that we are talking about and redirected by a vision to a different assignment. The key thing here is that Paul understood the leading of the Spirit. The people with him trusted his ability to hear the Voice of God, and also his ability to respond to that leading, no matter what form of leading the Lord chose.

THE ABIDING STRENGTH OF THE ANOINTING

> **Little children, it is the last time: and as ye have heard that antichrist shall come, even now are there many antichrists; whereby we know that it is the last time.**
>
> **They went out from us, but they were not of us; for if they had been of us, they would no doubt have continued with us: but they went out, that they might be made manifest that they were not all of us.**
>
> **But ye have an unction from the Holy One, and ye know all things.**
>
> **I have not written unto you because ye know not the truth, but because ye know it, and that no lie is of the truth.**
>
> **I John 2:18-21**

Anyone who is messing up their life, is messing it up on purpose. What John is trying to say to us here is that the anointing of the Holy Spirit, the anointing that Christ has anointed you with, is on the inside. Even without the baptism of the Holy Spirit externally on you, around you and over you, when you got saved, the Holy Spirit came inside of you to abide and to seal you to the day of redemption and you received an anointing inside of you. At that moment, you have the capability to know all things by the anointing. It gives the capacity for truth, not from an external source, so that you don't always have to have everything from the outside. When John says "you know all things," most of us would say we don't know all things. Now there will always be a couple of people who will say they know all things, but most of us know that in the natural we don't know all things. However, John is saying that by the anointing, the potential and capability for everything you need in the realm of knowledge is available to the believer inside, by the anointing of Christ. So when John said that you need no man to teach you, he is not saying that we know everything and don't need to come to church services or fellowship with the believers. What he means is that the anointing inside will teach you when you hear the truth from God's Word and it will bear witness with the Spirit of truth inside of you. He will reveal and produce clarity to what is being taught so that you receive insight. It is the anointing inside of you that produces the insight and helps you to receive and believe in what you have read and listened to as coming from God. A good example of this is the example of mothers with children. Mothers really don't have to go to a four-year college to know how to interpret the cry of their children. They can easily interpret the cry to mean time to eat, time to sleep or even time for attention. In all of these interpretations, they are usually ninety percent to a hundred percent right. If you ask the mothers how they know the interpretation of the cry, they will tell you that they don't know how, they just know from inside what it means. They have that anointing or unction inside of them, so they don't need anyone to teach them. They got it intuitively.

The anointing of the Spirit in you will communicate through your flesh, bearing witness to the Holy Spirit that is in you. That is why when you hear something taught that is Biblical and right, you say "Amen" because it is the Spirit in you that is revealing that, even if you have never thought about it. The anointing in you knows all things, but it does not mean that you know all things. It just means that with the Holy Spirit in you, you have the capacity in you at any moment to know anything that is knowable.

PITFALLS OF THE INWARD LEADING

The problem with this kind of leading is that it is the most mystical and the most subjective of all of the various ways God leads and directs. It is totally based on what you feel, what you sense, what you see and what you hear in your own spirit. When people say, "The Lord told me that we are to go there," by what you have just said or done, you have taken the leadership, or the Holy Spirit-inspired counselor, out of the process of counseling with you, because you have already appealed to the highest authority. This is the most dangerous form of leading because it is subjective, mystical and it is just what you feel. It does not give any boundaries to Scripture, to Godly counsel or any of the other ways God speaks. Anybody who always wants to do what they want to, will always tell you God has spoken to them to go there or to do that thing. Is it that God does not speak or cannot speak? The answer is, God is still speaking and will continue to speak to you and me. But we must be aware and watchful of the pitfalls in this way of leading because of the subjectivity and mysticism of this form of leading. That is why it is very important to check it with the other ways God leads for more clarity and insight.

Often the reason why most believers don't go to leadership or consult the other ways God speaks for more clarity, is that they are afraid that they will hear "No." If you are afraid that someone in leadership or one of the other forms of leading will produce red lights or say "No," then just admit to yourself that you really don't want to do the will of God. You just want to do what you want to do, because if you really want to do the will of God, the word "No" will never scare you. Anything as subjective as the inner leading of the Holy Spirit has to be properly balanced. When we study the context of I John 2, we will see the danger that is inherent in just following the Spirit subjectively. Jesus was able to follow the Spirit perfectly. He said I only do what I see my Father do. What was He talking about? He was not seeing the Father physically. He was seeing Him from inside His heart. He instinctively knew within how to react and what to do in every situation.

THE DANGER OF LIVING SUBJECTIVELY AND MYSTICALLY

> **Love not the world, neither the things that are in the world. If any man love the world, the love of the Father is not in him.**
>
> **And all they that heard it wondered at those things which were told them by the shepherds.**
>
> **I John 2:15, 18**

There are a lot of believers who live subjectively and mystically. If they see seven cars lined up in a row and they love the seventh one, they immediately conclude that is the car they should buy, because the number seven is God's number of perfection, or because they had a dream last night. Even though the dream is not a bad dream, you cannot be led by your dream ALONE. You must subject it to the other ways God speaks to produce accuracy and direction. There are a few more guide posts to line up before running off the cliff with a word from a dream. All the guide posts must be lined up.

Look at the Scripture that we just read. Why did John start by warning us not to love the world? When you are in love with God, walking with Him and abiding in Him, you instinctively know what to do. John is warning us that we are in a subjective area when operating in this form of leading. It can easily be confused with other things that come up inside, just like the spirits that are not of the Spirit. Why can't inner conviction be the place we stop? Because of the mixtures in us that can pollute and come up the same way as the Spirit of God. If our appetites were completely holy, pure and sanctified, we would be safe. But John went on to say in verse 18 that there is another anointing. It is not the Christ anointing. It is the antichrist anointing. Antichrist does not mean "against" Christ. It means "instead of" or "in place of." How do you identify this anointing? John said there are some things that you have to watch for, so that you don't get a false anointing. There are the antichrist spirits and these spirits are the lust of the flesh, the lust of the eyes and the pride of life. The lust of the flesh speaks of pleasure. It is to feel something. The lust of the eyes is the desire for possessions, to have something. The pride of life wants position, to be someone. These three can counterfeit the real anointing.

THE ANTICHRIST ANOINTING

Now there are three dimensions to self-gratification: to feel something, to have something and to be something. The devil has no new plans. He uses all of them against us. John says, "Watch out. Don't love these things. These loves and these affections can feel just like the leadings of God, because they are from within. That is an antichrist leading."

And the serpent said unto the woman, Ye shall not surely die:

For God doth know that in the day ye eat thereof, then your eyes shall be opened, and ye shall be as gods, knowing good and evil.

And when the woman saw that the tree *was* good for food, and that it *was* pleasant to the eyes, and a tree to be desired to make *one* wise, she took of the fruit thereof, and did eat, and gave also unto her husband with her; and he did eat.

Genesis 3:4-6

Let us look at a couple of examples. In the above Scripture, God instructed Adam not to eat of the fruit of the tree of the knowledge of good and evil. But the woman saw that the tree was good for food (pleasure) and she saw that it was a tree to be desired to make one wise and so it would be good to possess that possession. Then the serpent said that if you eat of it, you shall be as God; that is, be somebody (position). Right here are the three weapons in the satanic arsenal. There are no new tricks. They are always the same because they work. God is not against pleasure. He is not against possessions. He is not against position. If you humble yourself, God will exalt you. He is talking about illegitimate desires, illegitimate appetites that are in our flesh, and they feel just like the leading of the Holy Spirit.

And the men of Israel said, Have ye seen this man that is come up? surely to defy Israel is he come up: and it shall be, that the man who killeth him, the king will enrich him with great riches, and will give him his daughter, and make his father's house free in Israel.

I Samuel 17:25

In this Scripture, you find three things that King Saul promised or offered to the man who would go and fight against Goliath. The first thing he promised was his daughter in marriage, and this is symbolic of the desire for PLEASURE. Second, he promised to give the person who killed Goliath land to possess. He would make him a landowner. This is symbolic of the desire for POSSESSIONS. Finally, he promised to let the person who killed Goliath live tax-free. That is, the person's new position in Israel would be a tax-free POSITION. These are counterfeit motives to get somebody to fight the giant. Motives are what drive all of us. We need to be driven and motivated by the Holy Spirit. We need to know that whatever we are doing is motivated by and for the Holy Spirit and not by our flesh or our unmet needs. God uses motives and the devil uses motives. They both come from the inside, which makes it such a subtle deception. We must always make sure that we are led by the Spirit. However, there is another kind of leading and another kind of motive. It is counterfeit and it is rooted in these three desires.

And Jesus, when he was baptized, went up straightway out of the water: and, lo, the heavens were opened unto him, and he saw the Spirit of God descending like a dove, and lighting upon him:

Matthew 3:16

Then was Jesus led up of the Spirit into the wilderness to be tempted of the devil.

And when he had fasted forty days and forty nights, he was afterward an hungred.

And when the tempter came to him, he said, If thou be the Son of God, command that these stones be made bread.

But he answered and said, It is written, Man shall not live by bread alone, but by every word that proceedeth out of the mouth of God.

Then the devil taketh him up into the holy city, and setteth him on a pinnacle of the temple,

And saith unto him, If thou be the Son of God, cast thyself down: for it is written, He shall give his angels charge concerning thee: and in their hands they shall bear thee up, lest at any time thou dash thy foot against a stone.

Jesus said unto him, It is written again, Thou shalt not tempt the Lord thy God.

Again, the devil taketh him up into an exceeding high mountain, and sheweth him all the kingdoms of the world, and the glory of them;

And saith unto him, All these things will I give thee, if thou wilt fall down and worship me.

Then saith Jesus unto him, Get thee hence, Satan: for it is written, Thou shalt worship the Lord thy God, and him only shalt thou serve.

Matthew 4:1-10

This is another example. Jesus was baptized by John at the river Jordan and then was baptized in the Holy Spirit by the evidence of a dove coming upon Him. Afterward, He was driven by the Holy Spirit into the wilderness. While in the wilderness, Satan offered Jesus three things. The first thing he offered Jesus was to turn the stones into bread. This temptation tripped up the first Adam and caused him to eat the fruit, but it did not trip up the last Adam, Jesus. Jesus had no release in His spirit (in His inner guidance system) and so He said that man shall not live by bread alone, but by every word that proceedeth out of the mouth of God. He knew it was a set-up and He said no.

Second, the devil offered or promised Jesus all of the kingdoms and his glory for a possession. The subtle bait here is not just the possession, but the glory that comes out of the possession. Finally, the devil told Him to jump off the temple and that God would give His angels charge over Him. What he was actually saying was that he wanted Jesus to prove His position by jumping. Jesus refused because He knew His position and did not need to prove it. If you look at a fallen minister or a fallen believer, you will find these three things in their lives. Every one of them ran through red lights before they smashed up. We need to increase and improve our discernment so that a lot more people can arrive safely at their destination.

THE THREE GODS OF ISRAEL

In the nation of Israel, there were three false gods that plagued them throughout the entire Old Testament. They were Ashteroth, Baal and Molech. Ashteroth was the goddess of sex and pleasure. Baal was the goddess of increase (financial increase). People in the Old Testament understood then that there were ruling spirits over certain areas. A non-covenant Israelite would sneak out on his back property and build himself a little rock altar so that the high priests wouldn't see it. If they did, he would be stoned to death. He would make sacrifices to these spirits to appease and get the favor of Baal, so that she would bless his crops and he would prosper. But God hated the idolatry because they were looking to Baal for financial increase, instead of looking to God. Many Christians still do the same thing today.

Molech was the idol that had a furnace in its belly. People would offer their babies for the promise of promotion and elevation in the community. The root of Molech is the pride of life. Molech is the god of abortion. "I cannot have a baby because it is going to ruin my career. It is going to cramp my life."

The potential is unlimited to be led by the Holy Spirit. There is potential in every believer to know all truth and to be led by inner conviction, but the guard rails have to do with the watching out for the appetite. God can only lead you by holy, sanctified, pure desire and appetite. He will even use your desires to pull you into purpose and destiny. If you are abiding in Christ and delighting in the Lord, every desire you have in that position is going to be pure. The inner conviction always works when we are abiding in God. The problem is that sometimes we are in and sometimes we are out.

GOD SPEAKS THROUGH HIS WORD

God also speaks through His Word or through Scriptures. A lot of believers fail to really depend on God's ability to speak to them through His Word. They prefer a more "sophisticated" way. When God speaks to you through His Word, it is the same as a ministry gift coming to you and saying, "Thus saith the Lord." The degree of value that you place on the Voice of God released through His Word will produce the degree of change His Word will determine concerning what the Word is directed to do. I have noticed many times that when God speaks to us through His Word, that particular scripture or message from the Word tightly grabs hold of your spirit. Your spirit man leaps– just as the baby in Elisabeth's womb leaped when she came in contact with Mary. Your soul echoes a sound like that of a trumpet. You know for sure that God is speaking to you. In other words, that Scripture becomes personified and immediately connects to your spirit. Out of the *logos* leaps a *rhema* word sent directly to meet your immediate need.

> **All scripture is given by inspiration of God, and is profitable for doctrine, for reproof, for correction, for instruction in righteousness:**
>
> **II Timothy 3:16**

The Bible says all Scripture is given by inspiration. The Greek word for INSPIRATION is "OPNEUSTOS." It is only recorded once in the New Testament. It literally means "God-breathed," with the prefix "THEOS" meaning "God" and "PEO" meaning "breath." That gives us the insight to see that God breathed His truth into the hearts and minds of the writers of the Scripture. The Word of God is God HIMSELF speaking to us. We must take the Word spoken to us by God through His Word very seriously. The Word is the life of God. So when He speaks, He produces life in us, if we will move in obedience to His Word. We must pay great attention to this avenue or medium of God speaking. The Bible tells us the purpose of the Scripture being given: for doctrine, for reproof, for correction and for instruction. Let's just concentrate on two of these purposes: "correction" and "instruction." The word CORRECTION in the Greek is "EPANORTHOSIS." "ORTHOS" means "straight." The term suggests "restoration to an upright or a right state and improvement." Whenever God speaks to us through His Word to correct us, God is actually restoring us to an upright or to a right state.

INSTRUCTION comes from the Greek word "PADDY" which comes from "PAIS." This word means "child," and is also derived from the verb "PAD," which in classical Greek means "to train children." So the literal meaning of "PADDY" is "child training." But Biblical writers felt and understood that all effectual instruction for the sinful children of men includes and implies chastening. Since instruction is thought of as mainly intellectual, training is a more adequate translation. When God speaks to us, we must discover the purpose for which the Word has been directed. Is it for doctrine, reproof, correction or instruction in righteousness? Once we find out the purpose, then we must yield and allow God to have His way. We must accept His Word and allow His Word to fulfill His purpose in us.

My son, keep thy father's commandment, and forsake not the law of thy mother:

Proverbs 6:20

Thy word *is* a lamp unto my feet, and a light unto my path.

Psalm 119:105

God has a way of guiding His children. We want to live successful lives. We want to finish this life well. God has divine principles that He uses to keep us on course and navigate our lives, so that we can actually finish our life without making any unfortunate mistakes. It is possible to live life without any major mistakes. It is not possible as a human being not to make slight or minor mistakes, but the key thing is that it will not be fatal or a major mistake that ruins and destroys your life, the life of your family or your ministry.

THE MARRIAGE OF THE WORD AND THE SPIRIT

God's Word is for guidance. The Spirit plays a part, but not without the Word. The Word plays a part, but also not without the Spirit. The Word and the Spirit must be married to produce accurate and effective guidance.

> **In the beginning God created the heaven and the earth.**
>
> **And the earth was without form, and void; and darkness was upon the face of the deep. And the Spirit of God moved upon the face of the waters.**
>
> **And God said, Let there be light: and there was light.**
>
> **And God said, Let us make man in our image, after our likeness: and let them have dominion over the fish of the sea, and over the fowl of the air, and over the cattle, and over all the earth, and over every creeping thing that creepeth upon the earth.**
>
> **Genesis 1:1-3, 26**

When God wants to invade the physical realm, He has a classic pattern for doing it that is repeated over and over in Scriptures. What you will see is that sometimes you don't have an exact word or a particular verse in Scripture concerning your guidance, but you have a pattern in Scripture or you have principles in Scriptures. It is an agreement of His Word and His Spirit that God always uses. He will never lead you by the Spirit and be in disagreement with His Word. He will never give you a Word that disagrees with His Spirit. They will always work in perfect harmony. Now, notice in the Scripture that the Holy Spirit is hovering or brooding over a created world that is without order. God's desire is to invade it. How is He going to do it? Notice verse three. It says God said, "Let there be light and there was light." See how the Spirit and the Word worked together to impact the natural or the physical realm? Then, in verse 26 the Bible says, "then God said let us make man in our image, according to our likeness." In chapter 2, verse 7, we saw how God "formed man of the ground and breathed into his nostrils the breath of life and man became a living soul." What is the breath of life? The Spirit of God. When God was ready to make the world, the Spirit hovered over it. Then God spoke the Word and immediately order came out of confusion. Then He said, "Let us make man, that is His Word. And once man was made, God breathed into that man the Spirit of life and we have the creation of life.

When you are going to follow God, you must follow His Word and His Spirit. Make sure that these two are always in agreement. A lot of Christians spend their time in the Spirit. They emphasize the life in the Spirit. They can easily be deceived if they don't know the Word. For some reason, by the grace of God, they are very sensitive to the spiritual realm and sometimes they are right and sometimes they are wrong, but they don't know much Word. Then you have the other group of people that are much grounded in the Word and have no Spirit. Both extremes are wrong. Don't choose either of these. You want a balance of both in right harmony, if you follow the scriptural pattern. All Word and no Spirit causes you to dry up. You become a pharisee, an adherent to the letter of the law that kills. You become mean, legalistic and engender bondage without life. If you are all Spirit and no Word, you will become self-destructive and blow up. You will go nuts because you have no perimeters with which to bring order and you will have confusion. God is not the author of confusion, but of order. The combination of the Spirit and the Word will cause you to grow up. It is not one or the other. It is both in harmony to produce a mature Christian that has life and the right structure.

And the word of the LORD came unto me, saying,

Son of man, prophesy against the prophets of Israel that prophesy, and say thou unto them that prophesy out of their own hearts, Hear ye the word of the LORD;

Thus saith the Lord GOD; Woe unto the foolish prophets, that follow their own spirit, and have seen nothing!

Ezekiel 13:1-3

In this Scripture, God warns against the prophets who declare what they are saying to be from Him when actually it is not from Him. Then in verse 3, He says woe to the foolish prophets who follow their own spirit and have seen nothing. I am always afraid of immature Christians who are susceptible to the spirit realm. They don't know any Word, and someone who has a supernatural gift that is manifested through a familiar spirit can easily deceive them, because they don't know the Word. On the other hand, we don't want to be stuck on the Word without having any Spirit to give life and power and flow in the things of God. It is both of them. I have never met any Christian who doesn't lean more to one of these than the other. It does not mean that they are wrong, it is just their personal trait. It is how they were raised spiritually. It can always be adjusted and corrected to allow the flow of both. The adjustment and correction only happens when we are willing to respond to the spirit of change.

There is a principle in the Scripture where Jesus used wine and wineskins to illustrate the picture of the correspondence of the Word and the Holy Spirit to give us guidance. The Word corresponds to the wineskin. A wineskin holds the wine. It does not produce it. It just holds it. The new wine corresponds to the Holy Spirit. The wine (Holy Spirit) is alive. It is free flowing and powerful. To find its true expression, it cannot be left by itself. It has to come into a structure where it still has life, vitality, movement and power. The wineskin is the Word and the wine is the Holy Spirit. It is like a fountain pen. If I want to send a letter to my wife, I don't just get a piece of paper and a bottle of ink and just pour the ink on the writing paper and send it to her. She won't be able to read it. It is definitely ink and writing paper, but she still can't read it. If I put the ink (the wine, the Holy Spirit) in the pen (the structure, the Word) and it channels the expression of the Holy Spirit so that it does not limit its ability to form words and letters, then I can effectively communicate with her. Now it is doing its job. On the other hand, if the structure is so tight that the ink cannot come out, then I still cannot write. It is not one or the other. It is a balance. Sometimes in churches we just want the Spirit of God to flow and He is all over the place. Nobody can tell what He did because there was confusion everywhere and there was no order to that expression. The Holy Spirit is free, but He is still not without restraint. He has structure and He does not violate the Word. When the Holy Spirit operates within the structure of the Word, there is a release of direction, focus and impartation. The Spirit will get the job done. He flows through the structure of the Word. In the structure of the restriction of the Word, it gives us a limit, protection and balance. It is not to hinder you. It is to protect you.

THE WORD MADE ALIVE

In the beginning was the Word, and the Word was with God, and the Word was God.

The same was in the beginning with God.

And the Word was made flesh, and dwelt among us, (and we beheld his glory, the glory as of the only begotten of the Father,) full of grace and truth.

John 1:1-2, 14

Here we have the Word made alive in Jesus Christ. Did the Word by Himself do any miracle for thirty years? No. The Word by Himself did not do any ministry for thirty years. Why not? Ministry cannot be accomplished without the Spirit. How did God invade the natural realm with Jesus? First, He came with the Word to a woman, a virgin named Mary. He told Mary that she was going to conceive and that the Holy Child she was going to bring forth was going to be the Son of God. Now Mary got the Word, but she said, "How can this be?" which means that getting the Word alone does not make it happen. An Angel said, "The Holy Spirit will overshadow you and conception will take place." Now, notice the pattern again. When God created the world, the Holy Spirit hovered over it, God spoke the Word and order came. Then when God made man, He spoke the Word and said let us make man in our own image. Then He breathed into that dead form the Spirit of God and we have created life. The same thing happened when God sent Jesus. The Word became flesh and dwelt among us. He did not do any miracle and any ministry until the Spirit of God at the baptism of John came upon Him. Then He launched His ministry from that moment forth. We got the Word guided by the Holy Spirit, and the Spirit energizing His Word. The anointing of the

Word and the Spirit working in perfect harmony. Now, if you've got the Word in you and you've got the Spirit in you, you have the potential to walk like Jesus.

> **How God anointed Jesus of Nazareth with the Holy Ghost and with power: who went about doing good, and healing all that were oppressed of the devil; for God was with him.**
>
> **Acts 10:38**

How did this work in Jesus' ministry? The same way it is going to work in ours. The anointing of the Holy Spirit anointing the Word in us will cause the supernatural to be manifested. The guidance of the Spirit in Jesus' life was limited to the Father's will, nature, character and personality expressed in the written Word. Jesus never violated Scripture. He violated traditions and the Pharisees' rule, but not the Word and the Holy Spirit. Whenever you come in agreement with the Word and the Holy Spirit concerning a situation, you always get a solution. People often say "I feel led" or "I feel the Holy Spirit told me to do this." And often they are calling a misdirection a leading. The problem is that they are going outside what the Father would do, and the reason they do this is because they don't know what the Father would do, because they do not know the Word. The more you read the Word, the more you see how Father does what He does. The Word reveals God, reveals His nature, His character, what He likes and what He does not like, and the Scripture becomes our wineskin. The Scripture then gives definition to the expression of the Holy Spirit. It gives us limitations, guidelines and liberty, as well.

GOD SPEAKING THROUGH DREAMS AND VISIONS

This is another area that has created much controversy among the Body of Christ. There are those who believe that God speaks through dreams and visions, and there are others who greatly criticize and despise dreams and visions as avenues through which God speaks. Those that despise dreams and visions believe that their era is gone and that these are the times that God only speaks through His Word and through our recreated human spirit.

It is quite true that God speaks through His Word and through His Spirit. But it is also true that God still speaks through dreams and visions. It is unfathomable to say God does not speak through dreams and visions. I understand that dreams and visions have been greatly abused, but that does not mean we have to throw the baby out with the bathwater! We just need to understand God's ways!

The Church has not been properly taught about the operation, mechanism and interpretation of dreams and visions. It is a simple matter to have a dream or a vision. Yet it is another thing to understand what God is trying to convey to us and properly interpret it in the light and context of the Word. Every dream and vision must line up with the Word. Any dream and vision that does not line up with the Word of God is not worth considering.

But in order to understand and know whether a dream or a vision lines up with the Word or not, the believer must know how to interpret the symbolism of his dreams and visions. It is difficult for someone else to interpret your dream except that individual is prophetically led by the Spirit of God.

We must not depend totally on dreams and visions as the only way God speaks. If you don't have a dream or a vision, don't get upset. We must learn not to make a habit out of just wanting to have a dream or a vision. If it comes, it comes. It cannot be turned on. Dreams and visions must not be wrongly interpreted. If you don't understand your dreams or visions, ask your pastor or those who have been proven and gifted in the interpretations of dreams and visions.

Dreams and visions can come in various forms. Sometimes we get in very dangerous positions because we go to meetings and we hear men of God talk about what they have heard, how it came to them and then we try to lock the Spirit of God into a specific pattern or orbit. We hear popular ministers relate how God spoke to them, and a whole generation of ministers will try to go out by the arm of the flesh and create circumstances to duplicate what they've heard. Too many hear someone's testimony and think that God can only speak in that certain manner. Many of us end up fabricating fifty percent of what we say, and that is why we don't have results. The arm of flesh will never bring results. We must know that God can move through us uniquely. He does not have to move the same way with us as He moves with another person.

DREAMS

Sometimes in dreams things seen and heard are symbolic of the physical realm. The Old Testament is filled with vivid dreams. It is filled with dreams that have changed the destiny of men, cities, nations, and entire groups of people. Dreams are contained in the prophetic revelations of God. You don't have to be a prophet or a prophetic minister. But as a prophetic generation, there is an access to dreams that the Spirit of God reveals unto us for understanding. In the Old Testament, God communicated twenty-two times in dreams to His people. Dreams are those things that God reveals in the night seasons for the purpose of information and establishment.

> **For God speaketh once, yea twice, yet man perceiveth it not.**
>
> **In a dream, in a vision of the night, when deep sleep falleth upon men, in slumberings upon the bed;**
>
> **Then he openeth the ears of men, and sealeth their instruction,**
>
> **That he may withdraw man from his purpose, and hide pride from man.**
>
> **Job 33:14-17**

Dreams usually come during the sleeping hour. In slumbering or in deep sleep, God says He will visit in the dream to seal up the instruction of men. In other words, God opens up their eyes and then seals up their instructions. One of the greatest mistakes you can make is to always go to someone to help interpret your dreams and visions. Whenever you have a dream, the first thing you should do is to take some time to seek God for the interpretation after judging whether it is from God or not. There is always grace, and there is always an anointing and understanding made available whenever the Spirit of God speaks.

If there is not an interpretation for the dream, don't waste your entire life seeking for an interpretation when there is none. Don't waste your time trying to determine something that may not have any measure of validity in the Kingdom of God. Seek God for the interpretation and if the interpretation does not come, go on with the rest of your life.

> **And he said, Hear now my words: If there be a prophet among you, I the LORD will make myself known unto him in a vision, and will speak unto him in a dream.**
>
> **Numbers 12:6**

The Lord has promised to speak to His people through visions and dreams. In the Old Testament, great references were constantly made to the prophets. Thank God, that today, God is not partial. God is still speaking through dreams and visions to His prophets. But He is also speaking to the other five-fold ministry gifts and the entire Body of Christ.

Since this is the time of restoration, God is also restoring confidence in Holy Ghost-inspired dreams and visions. We must not totally depend or rely solely upon them, but we must see them as a viable avenue of communication. We've been subjected to erroneous teachings in this area, which has made most Christians reject the Word of the Lord that came through a dream or vision. And some, who are particularly gifted in this area, have withdrawn and won't share what they're dreaming. They are afraid of being criticized by other believers.

In some churches and groups, it is almost an abomination to say that God spoke to you in a dream or in a vision. It is acceptable to say that God spoke through His Word or through our recreated human spirit. But it is like a crime to say to someone that God spoke to you in a dream.

Dreams have been taught to be very unreliable. Many have lost confidence in their own dreams and can't tell whether they are from God or not. As a result of this, many have placed dreams on the back burner. God will continue to speak through any channel or source that He desires. The Body of Christ must be flexible and ready to receive the accurate Word of the Lord through whatever means it comes.

There are ministers who strongly teach and believe that the reason Christians dream often is because of what they eat, see on TV, watch in the movies, or experience during the day. While it is true that there are dreams that are not inspired or given by God, it is also true that some are given by God. The problem is not with the dream, but the problem is with the individual being able to discern if it is from God or not. There is more than a one-hundred percent chance for a man or woman, whose spirit man is developed, sensitive and uprightly walking before God, to accurately pinpoint if a dream is God-inspired or satanically inspired. Just because an individual does not have a personal experience with dreams, this should not make him criticize or doubt the credence of their existence.

> **And he dreamed, and behold a ladder set up on the earth, and the top of it reached to heaven: and behold the angels of God ascending and descending on it.**
>
> **And, behold, the LORD stood above it, and said, I am the LORD God of Abraham thy father, and the God of Isaac: the land whereon thou liest, to thee will I give it, and to thy seed;**
>
> **And thy seed shall be as the dust of the earth, and thou shalt spread abroad to the west, and to the east, and to the north, and to the south: and in thee and in thy seed shall all the families of the earth be blessed.**

And, behold, I am with thee, and will keep thee in all places whither thou goest, and will bring thee again into this land; for I will not leave thee, until I have done that which I have spoken to thee of.

Genesis 28:12-15

This is a great example of God speaking to an individual through a dream. Jacob, in going to take for himself a wife, had a dream while resting in the city of Luz. The dream showed the illustration of a ladder hooking up to heaven and the angels of God ascending and descending on it. Thank God for the existence and reality of angels today!

Jacob had the option to either believe that it was from God or not. The Bible lets us know that when Jacob woke up from his sleep, he knew surely the Lord was in that place. Jacob knew he had an encounter with God. He knew that God was speaking to him in the dream. He did not discard the Word of the Lord. He received God's Word, even though it came through the avenue of a dream. As the Body of Christ begins to walk and operate in the spirit of accuracy and sharpness, the Church will begin to accurately discern, understand and interpret what God is saying through dreams and visions.

God is still speaking today through dreams, just as He is speaking through other avenues and channels. God, in this restorative movement of His Spirit, is visiting the Church through dreams and visions. It is not that God will not speak through any other source and avenue, but during this end time, the Church will see, experience and hear God through all of His available channels and sources.

And Joseph dreamed a dream, and he told it his brethren: and they hated him yet the more.

And he said unto them, Hear, I pray you, this dream which I have dreamed:

For, behold, we were binding sheaves in the field, and, lo, my sheaf arose, and also stood upright; and, behold, your sheaves stood round about, and made obeisance to my sheaf.

And his brethren said to him, Shalt thou indeed reign over us? or shalt thou indeed have dominion over us? And they hated him yet the more for his dreams, and for his words.

And he dreamed yet another dream, and told it his brethren, and said, Behold, I have dreamed a dream more; and, behold, the sun and the moon and the eleven stars made obeisance to me.

And he told it to his father, and to his brethren: and his father rebuked him, and said unto him, What is this dream that thou hast dreamed? Shall I and thy mother and thy brethren indeed come to bow down ourselves to thee to the earth?

Genesis 37:5-10

Joseph had two dreams in which his destiny was being unfolded right before His eyes. God can unfold your destiny and show you what is to come through a God-inspired dream. Even though he was just a young seventeen-year-old boy, God, through dreams, showed Joseph what was ahead. God literally showed him his future. As Joseph in his innocence began to share his dreams, his brethren became enraged with him. It is important that you don't share your dreams with just everyone. There are folks who will kill your dream. Dreams should be shared with people with whom you are divinely connected, and not with just every Tom, Dick and Harry.

Even though Joseph's father and brothers were upset concerning the dreams, they were able to discern, understand

and interpret the meaning of the dream, although Joseph could not. The outcome of the dream was not manifested overnight, but in the process of time the dream was birthed from the spirit realm to the physical realm.

God will speak through any avenue or source He chooses. Most of the time, God will speak to an individual through an avenue that will be well understood and retained by that individual. Even though an individual may receive messages from his recreated human spirit and godly counsel, God, in cases of emergency and urgency, will speak to an individual through sources or channels with which they are familiar. He'll speak in a manner that they can easily discern, understand and fully interpret, until he or she is well developed in the other sources.

Most believers can easily detect when God is speaking to them because they've become skilled in one particular venue. Yet when God speaks through other manners, they find it much easier to disregard the message. They've become prejudiced and place God in a box, thinking that He'll only speak in one defined way. The Body of Christ in this generation, though they might have a specific avenue through which the Spirit of God speaks to them, will experience the Word of the Lord through every available avenue because God is going to reveal Himself in many dimensions.

Now let's see what the New Testament had to say about dreams. There are some Christians who strongly believe that dreams and visions are for the Old Testament Church and not for the New Testament Church.

> **Then Joseph her husband, being a just man, and not willing to make her a public example, was minded to put her away privily.**

But while he thought on these things, behold, the angel of the Lord appeared unto him in a dream, saying, Joseph, thou son of David, fear not to take unto thee Mary thy wife: for that which is conceived in her is of the Holy Ghost.

And she shall bring forth a son, and thou shalt call his name JESUS: for he shall save his people from their sins.

Then Joseph being raised from sleep did as the angel of the Lord had bidden him, and took unto him his wife:

Matthew 1:19-21,24

Joseph refused and would not believe the word from his wife Mary that was spoken to her by the Holy Spirit concerning her pregnancy and the birth of Jesus Christ. But he was able to believe and be persuaded by the angel of God who brought the Word of the Lord to him in a dream. Joseph had a God-inspired dream. Joseph could have said, "I don't believe in dreams." But that was not the case. The Bible says that he did everything the angel of the Lord bid him to do in the dream. That tells me that he was able to discern, understand and interpret the Word of the Lord from the dream. He obeyed the leading and the direction that he received through his dream.

And being warned of God in a dream that they should not return to Herod, they departed into their own country another way.

Matthew 2:12

In this case, the wise men were warned by God in a dream not to return to Herod. God spoke to the wise men concerning the plot, schemes and devices of King Herod toward the child Jesus in a dream. God instructed them not to return to Herod. This is an example of God speaking through dreams. The wise men believed God spoke to them. They did not ponder or doubt the message, but they discerned and understood that it was from God. They did not refuse the warning of God, even though it was through a dream. God is doing the same thing today. God is still warning, instructing, directing and promoting His people through the God kind of dreams. Yet there are believers who will not adhere to their dreams because they have rendered such messages unacceptable. But whether you personally like it or not, God will continually speak to His Church through any channel He pleases.

> **Then Joseph her husband, being a just man, and not willing to make her a public example, was minded to put her away privily.**
>
> **But while he thought on these things, behold, the angel of the Lord appeared unto him in a dream, saying, Joseph, thou son of David, fear not to take unto thee Mary thy wife: for that which is conceived in her is of the Holy Ghost.**
>
> **Matthew 1:19,20**

Again, the angel of the Lord appeared to Joseph in a dream after the death of King Herod, bringing a Word of the Lord for a new direction. God instructed Joseph to leave Egypt and go to Israel because there were people who wanted to kill the baby Jesus. New directions can be received through dreams. God will do and is doing the same thing today. There have been men and women who have been warned of impending accidents, plots, schemes and devices of the enemy through dreams. Restoration has begun. God is restoring everything back to His original state and condition.

CAUSES OF DREAMS

A lot of things can cause us to have dreams. One of them may be our activities during the day. We are more likely to dream of whatever has dominated our minds or thoughts throughout that day. Such dreams are not birthed from God, but from our personal activity.

Another way we can have dreams is that dreams can come from the "memory bank" of our personal history. Many times, it is quite possible that good and bad experiences of our past and present may surface and show up while we are unguarded in our sleep. God may use these times to bring clarity and healing to these unresolved issues and problems. However it will not be proper to say that it came directly from God. It actually came from the "bank" of our personal hurts and tragedies.

Dreams can also come to us as a revelation of the enemy's plan against our lives, families, ministries and churches. Sometimes we have nightmares, horrifying dreams, disturbing and terrifying dreams and visions. Often, we ignore them without taking the appropriate action in the Spirit realm. This type of dream is God exposing the attacks, plots and schemes by the devil that can be eradicated and thwarted by the prayer of faith. You may ask, "Why do I really need the dream? Why do I need to know what the devil is doing?" You see, knowing this is very helpful, because it will help to ignite your heart to wage war in the Spirit against the plans of the enemy. Instead of being afraid, depressed or discouraged in the attack, you can instead stand boldly and condemn the strategy and plot of the enemy.

God promises that in the last days He will pour out His Spirit upon all flesh; that our sons and daughters will prophesy and the young men will see visions and the old men will dream dreams. This is our confidence that we are in the last hour and that God is actually pouring out His Spirit. It is very important that you learn how to make the distinction between the dreams that are from God and those that are not, so that you may be able to interpret your dreams.

KEYS TO INTERPRETING DREAMS

Let's look at some keys that will help open the door to the interpretation of the dreams that God may give to you. Mind you, these are just "some" keys.

The first key is that you must have a one-to-one relationship with your Father. You must be in relationship with God and walking in His commandments to be able to understand what He is saying through dreams. The more depth you have with God, the more you'll become sharp and sensitive in understanding His Voice. If you don't have an ongoing relationship with God, you cannot have depth in the things of God. And if you don't have depth in the things of God, it becomes impossible to properly discern the Voice of God in dreams.

> **Yea, if thou criest after knowledge, and liftest up thy voice for understanding;**
>
> **If thou seekest her as silver, and searchest for her as for hid treasures;**
>
> **Then shalt thou understand the fear of the LORD, and find the knowledge of God.**
>
> **Proverbs 2:3-5**

The second key is that you must be ready and willing to research and investigate the symbols and sayings of the dream or revelation you receive. Many times, when we have a dream, it comes predominantly in symbols. Sometimes it does not come very clearly. This can be frustrating. If you really want to understand the meaning of the dream you receive and thereby know what God is saying to you, you must be ready to study and research the symbols of the dream. This is not for lazy people. Lazy Christians always want someone else to interpret their dreams for them. They are too lazy to take the time to research for themselves the meaning of the symbols in their dreams. The Bible says "If you call out for insight and cry aloud for understanding, and if you look for it as for silver and search for it as for hidden treasure, then you will understand the fear of the Lord and find the knowledge of God." This is the promise of God for us. Let's take advantage of it.

The third key is that whenever you receive a dream, the first thing you must do is to ask God if the dream is for you or for someone else. Many times, when you receive a dream, it can be for someone else in your family, among your friends, co-workers and church family or even someone with whom you're not familiar. It is important that you find who the dream is for, before you start panicking unnecessarily. People panic and become depressed and discouraged over dreams that are meant for others. The reason they feel this way is because they think it was for them. Be very careful and sensible in interpreting what you have seen. Don't even force an interpretation or try to make it fit a predetermined opinion or desire.

Finally, learn to honor others as you share what you have seen in your dream. Be ready and prepared to submit what you have seen and what you think it means to others who can help you arrive at a truthful and objective interpretation and thereby bring clarity to you.

HOW TO BE PREPARED TO RECEIVE A DREAM OR A VISION FROM GOD

I sleep, but my heart waketh: it is the voice of my beloved that knocketh, saying, Open to me, my sister, my love, my dove, my undefiled: for my head is filled with dew, and my locks with the drops of the night.

Song of Solomon 5:2

Often, you hear Christians say that they desire for God to speak to them in dreams and visions. Yet, they are not ready and prepared to receive when the dream or vision comes. It is important that we are in a ready posture or in a readiness of mind when we receive a dream or a vision. But how do we do that?

And I say unto you, Ask, and it shall be given you; seek, and ye shall find; knock, and it shall be opened unto you.

For every one that asketh receiveth; and he that seeketh findeth; and to him that knocketh it shall be opened.

If a son shall ask bread of any of you that is a father, will he give him a stone? or if he ask a fish, will he for a fish give him a serpent?

Or if he shall ask an egg, will he offer him a scorpion?

If ye then, being evil, know how to give good gifts unto your children: how much more shall your heavenly Father give the Holy Spirit to them that ask him?

Luke 11:9-13

First, ask the Lord to speak to you while you sleep and EXPECT Him to do it. Jesus said, "Ask and it shall be given to you." All you need to do is just ask with a sincere heart that God will speak to you while you sleep and He will.

Second, be willing, prepared and ready to wake up no matter how late in the night or in the morning to write down the things God reveals to you. Often, when God speaks to us in a dream or in a vision while we are sleeping, we get too lazy to wake up to write down what He reveals to us. Some of us just wake up and fall back to sleep. Yet you say that you want God to speak to you while you are asleep. There is a responsibility we must undertake when God speaks to us while we are asleep. We must train ourselves to be disciplined so as to be able to wake up and write down whatever God is revealing to us. Never be so lazy that you cannot treasure the Word of the Lord. One very important way to avoid laziness is not to eat too much before you go to bed. When you are filled up with food before going to bed, it makes it difficult for you to remember and receive what God is revealing to you.

Many of us have often awakened from a vivid dream in the middle of the night, thinking that we will remember it when the morning comes. When you do that, you will find yourself with a vague recollection of what the Lord had shown to you. This is why you must seize the moment.

Third, make a habit of keeping a pen and note pad at your bedside to inscribe those things you may receive, see and hear in your dreams and visions.

Finally, learn to make a note of your thoughts about the dream at the time. Then, when you awaken in the morning, you are then able to read it clearly and study it through to its interpretation. The very act of doing this will cause you to become more sensitive to hearing and receiving from the Lord while you sleep, which in turn will enable Him to speak more frequently to you this way.

VISIONS

Visions are another channel or source through which God can speak to His people today. Sometimes God can speak and lead a believer through a vision. There are three kinds of visions. The first kind is called the spiritual vision. The second kind is the vision which is received through a trance and the third kind is the open vision.

The spiritual vision is the vision that involves the ability to see into the Spirit realm. You are able to see with the eyes of your spirit. This has nothing to do with the physical eyes.

The second vision occurs when a believer falls into a trance. When a believer falls into a trance, his physical senses are suspended. In other words, they are not in charge of their physical senses. The spiritual senses take over. He or she is not unconscious; he or she is just unaware of his vicinity. He or she is more spiritually conscious than physically conscious.

The open vision is different. This is when all of your senses are intact. You can see the vision with your physical eyes. Your senses are not suspended. But the great difference is that only the individual sees what is going on. Nobody else within their surroundings sees what is going on except with the permission of the Spirit of God.

After these things the word of the LORD came unto Abram in a vision, saying, Fear not, Abram: I am thy shield, and thy exceeding great reward.

And Abram said, Lord GOD, what wilt thou give me, seeing I go childless, and the steward of my house is this Eliezer of Damascus?

And Abram said, Behold, to me thou hast given no seed: and, lo, one born in my house is mine heir.

And, behold, the word of the LORD came unto him, saying, This shall not be thine heir; but he that shall come forth out of thine own bowels shall be thine heir.

And he brought him forth abroad, and said, Look now toward heaven, and tell the stars, if thou be able to number them: and he said unto him, So shall thy seed be.

Genesis 15:1-5

Abram had a vision and received the Word of the Lord. Obviously, this was not a spiritual vision or a trance. Abram had an open vision. His senses were intact. They were not suspended. He knew in the vision that he was childless. If his senses were suspended, then he would not have known. But he knew what was going on around him. He knew that he had a steward named Eleazar. Abram was able to respond back to God in the vision and hold a conversation. This experience is not just for Abraham. God is doing the same thing today for all who will not limit Him. God wants also to speak and lead His people through visions. He desires to send His Word through any avenue He wills. We must not limit God. We will have visions like never before in these last days. But visions will come to those who believe that God still speaks through visions. They will not come to "doubting Thomases" or to the rigid, starchy and religious believers. They will only come to the sons of God that have been truly manifested in this hour. There are sons of God that have not yet been manifested and there are others who have. God is still waiting and yearning for His manifested sons.

And God spake unto Israel in the visions of the night, and said, Jacob, Jacob. And he said, Here am I.

And he said, I am God, the God of thy father: fear not to go down into Egypt; for I will there make of thee a great nation:

I will go down with thee into Egypt; and I will also surely bring thee up again: and Joseph shall put his hand upon thine eyes.

Genesis 46:2-4

Jacob, called Israel, had a vision in Beersheba when he came to offer sacrifices to God. He had an open vision in which God communicated with him. It is a beautiful thing for God to communicate to His people. God is still communicating with His people. Words of direction and prosperity were given to Jacob through visions. God, through a vision, will give new direction and leading to His people. There are many believers whose call was confirmed through a vision or a dream. I am not talking about man-made dreams and visions. I am referring to the God-inspired, God-given and God-directed vision and dream.

And it came to pass that night, that the word of the LORD came unto Nathan, saying,

Go and tell my servant David, Thus saith the LORD, Shalt thou build me an house for me to dwell in?

Now therefore so shalt thou say unto my servant David, Thus saith the LORD of hosts, I took thee from the sheepcote, from following the sheep, to be ruler over my people, over Israel:

I will be his father, and he shall be my son. If he commit iniquity, I will chasten him with the rod of men, and with the stripes of the children of men:

But my mercy shall not depart away from him, as I took it from Saul, whom I put away before thee.

And thine house and thy kingdom shall be established for ever before thee: thy throne shall be established for ever.

II Samuel 7:4,5,8,14,15,16

The prophet Nathan had a similar experience. He had a vision from God, not for himself, but for King David. The Lord can give us a vision for someone other than ourselves. God spoke to the prophet Nathan in a vision confirming David's kingdom through his sons, promising eternal mercy and kingdom to the house of David. This is what God can do through a vision. We can receive accurate Words of the Lord from a vision for our brothers and sisters. Visions are not meant to heap glory and praise upon ourselves. We must never become conceited or develop a "big head," for the dreams and visions are an act of God.

God knows us better than we know ourselves. He will not give a vision to someone just so he can go and proclaim "I just heard from God!" Instead, God will give a vision or speak to those He knows will follow Him out of obedience. It is only as we develop a faithful and obedient heart, that God can trust us to hear Him when He speaks.

God is looking for those to whom He can speak in the midnight hour and say, "Go and lay your hands on that sister," and they will obediently get out of bed and go straight to that sister's house. God does not give an individual a vision or a dream or even speak to an individual so they can go around rejoicing how wonderful it is that God spoke to them. God will only give visions, dreams and instructions to an individual that will be obedient to His Voice once he or she hears it.

Again, let's look at visions in the New Testament.

And he became very hungry, and would have eaten: but while they made ready, he fell into a trance,

And saw heaven opened, and a certain vessel descending unto him, as it had been a great sheet knit at the four corners, and let down to the earth:

Wherein were all manner of fourfooted beasts of the earth, and wild beasts, and creeping things, and fowls of the air.

And there came a voice to him, Rise, Peter; kill, and eat.

Now while Peter doubted in himself what this vision which he had seen should mean, behold, the men which were sent from Cornelius had made inquiry for Simon's house, and stood before the gate,

Acts 10:10-13,17

Peter fell into a trance, which is another form of vision. As we said earlier, what at times is seen and heard in a vision is symbolic. It takes the Spirit of God to properly interpret a symbol. That is why it is important not to share your vision with just anybody. It should only be shared with people whom the Spirit of the Lord specifies. They should be men and women that are gifted in properly interpreting your vision.

Peter saw heaven open and he saw a certain vessel descending to him. In other words, Peter saw things that he could not understand. Many of us have visions and dreams like that. We see things that we cannot understand. We cannot tell what it means. We cannot even relate to it. So what we do is, we just abandon the vision or dream in our minds. It is important that we learn to write our visions and dreams in a diary, whether we understand them or not. This is necessary because sometime in the future, you will be surprised how that vision or dream will unfold before your eyes.

Peter could not understand his trance. The Bible says that Peter was perplexed concerning the meaning of the trance. He literally was unable to interpret his vision. While he was still pondering about it, the interpretation was made clear when Peter arrived at the house of Cornelius, who was a Gentile. Peter said in verse 28, "You know that it is an unlawful thing for a man that is a Jew to keep company, or come unto one of another nation; but God has shewed me that I should not call any man common or unclean."

ANOTHER DIMENSION

Where there is no vision, the people perish: but he that keepeth the law, happy is he.

Proverbs 29:18

Without a prophetic vision the people perish. Another translation says, "Without a prophetic vision, the people cast off restraint, without a prophetic vision, the people cast off discipline, and without a prophetic vision, the people wander in darkness." Where there is a prophetic vision, there is a harness directive. I believe that in the last days, God will raise up young men which have visions for the Body of Christ to bring restraint upon the Body of Christ and to mobilize us to the will of God.

I believe old men will rise up with dreams. We often talk about how Martin Luther King, Jr. stood up and said, "I have a dream." What was it? Do you believe it was something that came to him in the night? Do you believe it was something that came before him in a trance? No. I believe it was the quickening power of God that wanted to use a man to reveal the destiny of a nation, to break down strife, to break sectarianism, to break down racism and bring a nation into the position of divine unity.

So there is another whole aspect where God can release a purpose in a man and the man can rise up and say, " I have a dream and the dream will come upon the people for restraint and for discipline to bring the people together." The fulfillment of Acts 2:14 rests upon us. It does not rest upon some mystical time clock out in the heavens somewhere. It rests upon a generation that will arise and take upon themselves the restraint and the discipline of the Holy Spirit to prepare for the last day visitation of God's Spirit and glory.

GUIDELINES FOR INTERPRETING DREAMS, VISIONS AND TRANCES

Dreams, visions and trances come to us in symbolic forms. Seldom do they come to us plain and clear without any symbolic meaning. The majority of dreams, visions and trances come in symbols, and because of this it is very important to understand the guidelines for interpreting them.

The first step is to rightly determine which elements or parts of the dream, vision or trance are meant to be interpreted as symbolic. If the picture or language of the dream, vision or trance makes no literal or actual sense, then it must be interpreted as having symbolic sense. If it does make literal or actual sense or meaning, then it can only be interpreted as having symbolic sense or meaning when the dream, vision or trance implies or relates to other dreams, visions or trances that you have had.

Second, the interpreter of the dream, vision and trance must be able to recognize the three fundamental elements of symbolic interpretation. That is, the significance of a symbol is based upon the literal or actual nature and characteristic of that which is being used as a symbol. A symbol is meant to represent something different than itself. The interpreter must understand that the link between that which is used as a symbol and that which is symbolized is the characteristic common to both.

Third, the interpreter must keep in mind that something may be used to symbolize more than one thing in a dream, vision or a trance. The same symbol may represent different aspects of a characteristic. For example, the picture of gold is used to represent divine nature, wisdom or faith. Also some symbols may have good and evil aspects to them. For example, the lion is used as a symbol of Jesus, His saints and also the devil in Revelation 5:5 and I Peter 5:8. Symbols often have negative and positive or good and bad applications. For example, birds, such as the dove or raven, symbolize spirits. The dove is symbolic of the Holy Spirit and the raven is symbolic of the evil spirit, yet both are birds. Remember, there is one interpretation but many applications of symbols. It is worth remembering that Satan is the great counterfeiter of all that God does. He is not an originator, but a counterfeiter. God is the originator of all things, while Satan counterfeits all that God does. The true believer is not to let the error of cultic symbolism rob him of the truth of divine symbolism. The Bible provides safe guidelines for principles of interpretation of those symbols which the believer should follow. This will prevent you from falling into any counterfeit symbolism or false allegories in your dream, vision or trance.

GOD SPEAKING THROUGH PROPHETIC WORDS

Many Christians actually believe that this ended years ago. Some don't even think God speaks through a prophetic word. Some groups of believers think that the era of the prophetic is gone. Let me tell you, the prophetic is very real today! God is bombarding His Body with prophetic words. There are those that will hear the sound and there are others that will not, because of their traditions and refusal to listen.

Despise not prophesyings.

I Thessalonians 5:20

The Bible says we should not despise prophesying. Prophesying is crucial and critical to the Body of Christ. We need the Word of the Lord. We need it in our meetings and in our individual lives constantly. I am not talking about words that are not lined up with the Bible. Every prophetic word that is given, must be under the authority of the written Word of God. If someone says, "Thus saith the Lord," and the word is not in harmony and in conjunction with the written Word of God, it should be rejected.

Also, we cannot always open the Bible and find out specifically where to go and what to do in every situation of life. Specific needs for guidance and direction often require specific words from God. There is not always specific Scripture that will tell you to buy a car or not to buy a car. In the process of studying and reading the Bible, one might find principles that relate to the issue, but no specific word as to whether to buy the car or not.

I remember many years ago, when I was in Nigeria, my homeland, I battled over certain decisions to make. This continued for some time. I went to the Word and began to study until I got direction concerning the decision. Still, it did not seem that the direction was clear because it was not specific. One Sunday morning, I went to a church that I had never been to before. I did not know the pastor of the church. As I walked into the church while the pastor was preaching, all of a sudden the pastor stopped and said, "Young man, thus saith the Lord..." to me. It was specific. It was sharp and accurate and it pinpointed my problem and the solution. That was a prophetic Word from God. It made my direction clear.

We must embrace what God is doing in the land. We must flow with it. Many times we don't understand the prophetic, but we have a knowing inside of our spirit that the prophetic is real and is true. That's all right. Let's go with it until we fully understand it. Get eager for the prophetic Word of God! When it comes, embrace it and cherish it, because it has the power to change your destiny for good and not for evil.

PROPHETIC CONFIRMATION

And now, behold, I go bound in the spirit unto Jerusalem, not knowing the things that shall befall me there:

Save that the Holy Ghost witnesseth in every city, saying that bonds and afflictions abide me.

But none of these things move me, neither count I my life dear unto myself, so that I might finish my course with joy,

and the ministry, which I have received of the Lord Jesus, to testify the gospel of the grace of God.

Acts 20:22-24

Here in the Scripture we find that Paul, before his arrival at Jerusalem, received prophetic words concerning what was to befall him in Jerusalem. This Word of the Lord that came to Paul did not come from his inner witness or voice. It was a prophetic word that was spoken to him by people in every city. Prophetic confirmation is a valid form of God conferring His will on certain matters. It is the least used of all of the various guidance systems of God, but it is still extremely valid. Actually, you are going to find it used a great deal in Scripture for exhortation, encouragement and edification. The principles that override all of these guidance systems are: when you want to find direction, God says line up two or three at a minimum. Obviously, the more important the decision, the greater the risk involved and the more confirmation that you want. It is not Lotto. It is not random choice and luck. God really wants you to know how to be led. There will always be an element of risk in doing the will of God, because He loves faith. However, it is not presumptuous risk. It is not silly and stupid risk. It is the risk that is based on Scripture, a witness in your spirit, wise counsel and all of God's guidance systems lining up. You still have to have the courage to take the step of faith. You are not going to get yourself into any dangerous trouble, if you are obeying the will of God.

PROPHETIC GUIDELINES

How is it then, brethren? when ye come together, every one of you hath a psalm, hath a doctrine, hath a tongue, hath a revelation, hath an interpretation. Let all things be done unto edifying.

If any man speak in an unknown tongue, let it be by two, or at the most by three, and that by course; and let one interpret.

But if there be no interpreter, let him keep silence in the church; and let him speak to himself, and to God.

Let the prophets speak two or three, and let the other judge.

If any thing be revealed to another that sitteth by, let the first hold his peace.

For ye may all prophesy one by one, that all may learn, and all may be comforted.

And the spirits of the prophets are subject to the prophets.

For God is not the author of confusion, but of peace, as in all churches of the saints.

If any man think himself to be a prophet, or spiritual, let him acknowledge that the things that I write unto you are the commandments of the Lord.

But if any man be ignorant, let him be ignorant.

Wherefore, brethren, covet to prophesy, and forbid not to speak with tongues.

Let all things be done decently and in order.

I Corinthians 14:26-33, 37-40

This Scripture gives us some prophecy guidelines. This is a spectacular gift, but also the most dangerous. When it is right, it is powerful. But when it is wrong, it can be devastating to people and leave them shattered, so be very careful and serious when you approach this method of guidance. In the above Scripture, Paul is correcting the church that is misusing spiritual gifts and creating confusion.

The early Corinthian church had all of the power, all of the anointing and all of the gifts of the Spirit. Most of Paul's letter is not to take away the gift, but to correct the abuse and the misuse of the gift. There is structure and there is freedom. The Holy Spirit is the liquid (wine) and the freedom. The Word of God is the wineskin and the structure. The Spirit operates within the structure of Scripture because He is not the author of confusion.

> **But he that prophesieth speaketh unto men to edification, and exhortation, and comfort.**
>
> **How is it then, brethren? when ye come together, every one of you hath a psalm, hath a doctrine, hath a tongue, hath a revelation, hath an interpretation. Let all things be done unto edifying.**
>
> **My love be with you all in Christ Jesus. Amen. The first epistle to the Corinthians was written from Philippi by Stephanas and Fortunatus and Achaicus and Timotheus.**
>
> **I Corinthians 14:3, 26, 29**

Now look at the Scripture. Edification builds up, exhortation encourages and stirs you to obey the will of God, and comfort will stir you up, especially in time of trouble and trials. Understand that this is going to be the purpose of God. God does not give us a gift so that we can have a spiritual orgasm and feel good. He gives it to build up the Body. Everything in God is redemptive. Even when He disciplines and corrects you, it is also to redeem His purpose in you. It is not to drive you away or to hurt you. It is to correct you so you can fulfill the good purpose in you. The end result of all legitimate New Testament prophecy is comfort. It does not matter the channels or the forms of the release of it. Its ultimate destination will be to produce comfort. That is why the Holy Spirit is called the Comforter. When you are wrong,

He is going to rebuke you or discipline you, but it will never be to destroy you. The end result will always be a promise of comfort. Prophetic confirmations have to have guidelines like every other gift. In verse 29, Paul says let the prophets prophesy, but let their words also be judged. There is freedom, but there is also structure. All prophecy in the New Testament must be judged. I don't care how many books you have written. I don't care about the notoriety you carry as a prophet; your words still must be judged. Every prophetic word in the New Testament is commanded to be judged because in the Old Testament, if a prophet prophesied something from God and it did not come to pass, they were killed. What they spoke had to come to pass or he was a false prophet and he was sentenced to death.

In the New Testament, you judge the prophecy or the prophetic word released to you. You don't judge the prophet and sentence him to death when his prophetic words don't come to pass. Instead, you judge the prophecy and, if it is not in line with the Word or with the Spirit of the Word, you then sentence the prophetic word to death. How? By rejecting it and refusing to walk in it. We must understand that in the New Testament, this gift flows through a vessel. The vessel is often imperfect and because of the imperfection of the vessel, it is important to judge the prophetic words by the standard of the Word and of the Spirit. You can be an immature vessel and have a very powerful gift. The gift does not validate your maturity. You can be a baby and have a gift. So you have to judge it, lest you run off thinking, "Well God said." When you are judging, you are not judging the prophet. You are judging his words. If a prophet is intimidated by having his word judged, then he is not a mature man and he is in error.

If you are angry because you came to leadership or eldership and said "I believe the Lord is saying ...," and leadership said "We believe you should hold that for now," or "It is not the right time to embark on it" or you were told that what you received did not flow with the Word or the Spirit of the Word after it had been fully examined by leadership, if you got mad, upset and refused to abide, then you have just set yourself up for a big disaster. That is why it is important that you are planted in the right local church, where the leadership is mature in the things of the Spirit and you trust in the anointing that they carry.

KINDS OF PROPHECY

When thou art departed from me to day, then thou shalt find two men by Rachel's sepulchre in the border of Benjamin at Zelzah; and they will say unto thee, The asses which thou wentest to seek are found: and, lo, thy father hath left the care of the asses, and sorroweth for you, saying, What shall I do for my son?

I Samuel 10:2

Neglect not the gift that is in thee, which was given thee by prophecy, with the laying on of the hands of the presbytery.

I Timothy 4:14

There are other kinds of prophecy. There is the directional prophecy. These are very tame. You don't find much of this in the New Testament. In the above Scripture, you see an example of directional prophecy. Here the prophet Samuel tells Saul what to do, where to go and what to expect when he gets there. There is also the conferral prophecy. This is when a gifting is conferred on a man by the Holy Spirit through the laying on of hands and prophecy.

There is the correctional prophecy and there is the judgment prophecy. These are all biblical. In Acts 5, Peter, Ananias and Sapphira experienced this kind of prophecy. Peter prophesied judgment for the disobedience of Ananias and Sapphira and they died instantly. The problem with this form of prophecy is that it is dangerous when it is unchecked. However it is a valid means of confirmation when used within the perimeter of the Word and the Spirit of the Word.

Where no oxen are, the crib is clean: but much increase is by the strength of the ox.

Proverbs 14:4

Often because people are scared of the supernatural and afraid to embrace the gifts of the Spirit. They opt for a clean stall. Then there is no power, no Holy Ghost manifestation, and no force to produce an increase, just intellectual transmittal of information. As a result, they have a clean stall but have no life. If you get an ox in real agriculture, it can produce a lot for you, but you will have to clean up a little bit of mess occasionally. If the anointing is flowing and I allow biblical government, biblical relationship and biblical gifts to exist, there will be an occasional potential for wrong. If you give the freedom and right to speak, then you have to give a Nazi skinhead the right to speak also, because freedom of speech also includes what they have to say. This is in spite of how I detest what they have to say. The same law that gives you freedom, gives the evil freedom, too. So God puts in the Church guidelines and governments to take care of that. I cannot prohibit it from happening, but I can prohibit it from damaging anything. When we want the oxen to produce an increase, we must be ready and willing to embrace the fact that along with the increase may come some level of mistakes.

CONFIRMATIONS THROUGH PROVISIONS

And the word of the LORD came unto him, saying,

Arise, get thee to Zarephath, which belongeth to Zidon, and dwell there: behold, I have commanded a widow woman there to sustain thee.

So he arose and went to Zarephath. And when he came to the gate of the city, behold, the widow woman was there gathering of sticks: and he called to her, and said, Fetch me, I pray thee, a little water in a vessel, that I may drink.

I Kings 17:8-10

For I am the LORD, I change not; therefore ye sons of Jacob are not consumed.

Malachi 3:6

Provision is one way God navigates us toward His assigned destination. According to a survey, the favorite Scripture of Christians and non-Christians alike is from the 23rd Psalm. God is a good God and He is a God of provision. If God is guiding, then God will provide all that is needed. The ultimate confirmation of whether we are on track with God is this principle: Is God providing? It is a practical demonstration of God's guidance when there is provision for you in what He has called you to do. The Bible is filled with remarkable events that this is true. When God commanded Noah to build an ark, He gave Noah the wisdom and knowledge to build it, because there were no ships available to pattern it after and there was no ocean. There had never been any flood or rain experienced. By faith he had to build the ark. Second, God had to provide the resources to do it. He had to get the lumber and all of the other necessary things that were needed to build a ship or an ark of that magnitude.

Then above all, He had to provide a hundred and twenty years to finish the job. God not only gave him the resources and the know-how to build it, He also gave Noah the time to build it.

This is very important to understand. Whatever God called you to do, whatever your purpose is on this earth, God will give you the amount of time in your life to do what you are called to do. Paul said "I have finished my course." Jesus said, "It is finished." You cannot say that or do that if you do not know that what you are called to do is completed. God can lengthen your years to accomplish your destiny. You and I can shorten it by our disobedience and rebellion. God will give you the time to accomplish what He has ordained for you. Circumstances and the facts don't count when God makes a promise to you. That is why it is good that you know the will of God for your life. That means that, if the doctor says that it could be malignant, well it could be. But it won't kill you if it takes your lifetime to fulfill the assignment and it has not yet been fulfilled. Even that bad report will not be able to stop you. God will either heal it or hold it in check. He will not let you die prematurely without fulfilling what He has called you to do. A sense of destiny will eliminate fear. When you know where you are going and you are quite aware that you are instructed to go that way by God, nothing in hell can take you out. Only your disobedience, rebellion and a life that does not line up with the Word and the Spirit of the Word can take you out.

When God delivered Israel from Egypt and led them through the wilderness, He sent manna from heaven. He made water come from a rock. If God is taking you into a difficult place, He will provide for you, even if He is disciplining you or He is putting you into a prison, like Joseph. He will provide everything you need– the grace, the finances, and the ways will be provided for you to accomplish what He has ordained. You don't have to know how. He will provide. The greatest provision story in Scripture has to be Genesis chapter 22 in which our salvation and the purchase of it by Jesus Christ is foreshadowed with a beautiful story of Abraham, a father having an only begotten son conceived when he was a hundred years old. God called him to a mountain to sacrifice his son and there his son Isaac gathered the wood and the fire. He said to his father that he had the wood and the fire, but where was the sacrifice? Abraham speaking by faith said God will provide Himself an offering. And just before the knife entered Isaac's chest, God stopped Abraham's hand. In Isaac's stead God provided a ram as a sacrifice. God uses provision as one of the ways He guides His children.

Watchman Nee, who wrote many books and was confined to solitary for twenty years by the Communist Chinese, said that provision is one of the first methods God uses to restrain his overzealous servants who are getting beyond the will of God for their lives. He pulls the rug of provision out from under them. God, if He does not want me somewhere, can withhold the provision for that thing. Restraint is one way God can hold you back from what is not the center of His will. Don't volunteer for somebody else's call. You will starve to death. Provision is only meant for the individual that is assigned to the call. God promises to provide as He called you and as you are being led by His Spirit, not as you are volunteering to go your own way. He made no such promise. There is a timing of God even when you are called by God. If He is guiding, He will be providing everything that you need. If your well is dried up, one of two things is happening: either God is moving you, or you missed God and you are not where you are supposed to be. God provides when He guides you somewhere. It is not how much you know or how well you can preach. It is not how well you are anointed. You can be anointed from your head to your toes and yet He did not call you to what you are doing. I am not saying that there will not be trials and temptations against your calling. But despite the trials, the pressure and the temptation, when you are called to do a thing, whether it is on a small scale or large scale, He will see you through the trials, pressure and temptation and bring you to a place of provision where the vision is fulfilled, or where you are progressing toward the vision. The call is in direct proportion to your provision. The key thing is, make sure you are called to what you are doing. You can have more anointing than everybody in a whole city, but if God did not call you, you will not get a dime. You will end up starving.

RESPONSIBILITY OF HEADSHIP

> **But if any provide not for his own, and specially for those of his own house, he hath denied the faith, and is worse than an infidel.**
>
> **I Timothy 5:8**

> **Night and day praying exceedingly that we might see your face, and might perfect that which is lacking in your faith?**
>
> **II Thessalonians 3:10**

The first assignment of a husband is to provide for his family. If God is not coming through for me and I have been called to a ministry, then there is a problem. If it is a season of trial or attacks that you are facing, then it is a different story. The husband provides for his family. God is our husband and He provides for us when we are doing what He has assigned us to do. God wants to get the sluggard and the lazy man's attention by lack of provision. He says if he won't work, no provision will be provided. We are not talking about handicapped people or a disadvantaged, underprivileged person. We are talking about able, strong and lazy people. There are people that want to work and yet cannot find a job. That is a different case. We are talking about Christians in the Church that are so lazy and really do not want to do anything with their lives.

> **And the word of the LORD came unto him, saying,**
>
> **Get thee hence, and turn thee eastward, and hide thyself by the brook Cherith, that is before Jordan.**
>
> **And it shall be, that thou shalt drink of the brook; and I have commanded the ravens to feed thee there.**
>
> **So he went and did according unto the word of the LORD: for he went and dwelt by the brook Cherith, that is before Jordan.**
>
> **I Kings 17:2-5**

Now watch this. Here we have the prophet Elijah who has just confronted Ahab and Jezebel and then pronounced three years of drought without rain. In the midst of what is going on, God spoke to him concerning a new direction. God told him where to go, but he also let him know that when he gets there, he will know He sent him there because there will be water to drink and food to eat. In other words, Elijah would know God is sending him there because there will be provision for the assignment. An important thing to note is that when God gives you direction, it may be strange or it could be an obscure place like the brook Cherith. One of the many ways you will know that it is God is that there will be provision.

Notice how he got his provision. Through a raven. God is the Lord of clean birds and unclean birds. A raven is a dirty bird. God would not allow a raven to be used in any sacrifices because it is termed unclean. The lesson here is that you can miss your blessing if you reject the container it comes in. It may not come in a charismatic container. It may not come in the one you like and honor. It might not even be a Christian that God uses to provide your need, and it will be as much God as it would be if Billy Graham sent you a check. He may use the federal government. He can use anything He wants to use. He owns the whole earth and everything in it. God is over the lost and the believer. To fulfill a purpose, He can touch their heart and move on their will so that they don't know why they are even doing what they are doing. In this story, it was not the devil that dried up the brook. It was God Himself. Elijah, when he moved to the "Cherith Hotel," had his Sony Walkman out there. He had his tapes and had Domino's Pizza delivery morning and night. He was having a good time. He was not ready to go anywhere and I would not blame him if he didn't. It was a comfortable hotel. While there was famine in the whole land, he was enjoying the plush hotel of Cherith. God knew that Elijah was not going to move, so God dried up the brook. Then Elijah had to move. It is not always the devil that dries up our well. It can be God, so as to give a new marching order to start moving. Very little in your Christian life will be permanent. The brook can be dried up for you and not for the next person standing by you. When it happens, it is not time to judge or extend any kind of condemnation. It is just a response to a new marching order and that might not apply to the next person standing by you.

And the word of the LORD came unto him, saying,

Arise, get thee to Zarephath, which belongeth to Zidon, and dwell there: behold, I have commanded a widow woman there to sustain thee.

So he arose and went to Zarephath. And when he came to the gate of the city, behold, the widow woman was there gathering of sticks: and he called to her, and said, Fetch me, I pray thee, a little water in a vessel, that I may drink.

I Kings 17:8-10

In preparation for further guidance in the life of Elijah, God had to take the provision away. In the scripture above, "Arise and go" is the command and the promise that, if you do what I say and go where I am telling you, I have already in advance of your coming taken care of your needs. Elijah obeyed God and it was confirmed just as God promised him. While God was preparing him, He was also preparing the widow. God does not send His servants to places where they starve to death. You can take a trip God never authorized and you will pay dearly for it.

For I am the LORD, I change not; therefore ye sons of Jacob are not consumed.

Malachi 3:6

Jesus Christ the same yesterday, and to day, and for ever.

Hebrews 13:8

There is a consistency in God and one of the consistencies is that He changes not. He is consistent and does not change. That means that if He was the Provider in the Old Testament, He will be the same to us today. He does not change. Men change the doctrine. Men change everything, but He does not change. The problem is that we seek guidance from God, instead of the God of guidance. That means there are people who need counseling, who have no personal prayer life. They do not want to pray and learn how to seek the Lord. They just want their answers. They want you to tell them what they need to do. They see the answers, instead of the big solution which is God Himself. Malachi chapter three is about the fathers of Israel going away from God. God said "return to Me and I will return to you," and they said how will we return to You? The Lord operates in seasons of provision. The guidance principles don't substitute for the God of guidance. When I am talking about provision as a guidance factor here, I am talking about an obedient Christian. God will not confirm disobedience. If you are robbing God and not seeking Him, He is not going to confirm what you are doing.

THE PEACE OF GOD

For as many as are led by the Spirit of God, they are the sons of God.

Romans 8:14

This is the third time I am coming to you. In the mouth of two or three witnesses shall every word be established.

II Corinthians 13:1

This is another form of God's guidance system. God can guide you by His peace. However, never forget that you cannot just go by the peace of God alone to be led. You have to have at least two or more witnesses before God's leading is established. You are going to make a mistake if you just take one element of guidance to the exclusion of the others. God says get two or three of them to agree at a minimum on a major decision before you move. If you do, you will move safely, you will move with protection and there will be no fatal consequences to you at all. Where most believers make mistakes is taking just one of these channels of leading or guidance to an extreme and excluding the other guidance principles or channels of leading.

That at that time ye were without Christ, being aliens from the commonwealth of Israel, and strangers from the covenants of promise, having no hope, and without God in the world:

But now in Christ Jesus ye who sometimes were far off are made nigh by the blood of Christ.

For he is our peace, who hath made both one, and hath broken down the middle wall of partition between us;

Ephesians 2:12-14

And you, that were sometime alienated and enemies in your mind by wicked works, yet now hath he reconciled

Colossians 1:21

And let the peace of God rule in your hearts, to the which also ye are called in one body; and be ye thankful.

Colossians 3:15

Therefore being justified by faith, we have peace with God through our Lord Jesus Christ:

Romans 5:1

There are two kinds of peace mentioned in Scripture. There is the peace with God and there is the peace of God. The peace with God is the benefit, the privilege and the gift of every one who has accepted Jesus Christ as his or her personal Savior. Peace with God is your benefit. Before we became Christians, we were enemies of God. We did not think like Him or act like Him. We were self-seeking. Our salvation is the result of Christ dying on the Cross, taking the sentence of death in His own flesh for our sins and redeeming us. Jesus said, "It is finished." God is satisfied with what Jesus did. If you accept what Jesus did, He will put you in Christ legally. This gives us peace with God.

Now the other concept of peace is the peace of God. Peace with God is salvation, and peace with God makes possible the peace of God inside the believer. The peace of God becomes a guidance system for those at peace with God. It can guide you in decisions, directions for your life and relationships.

> **For the kingdom of God is not meat and drink; but righteousness, and peace, and joy in the Holy Ghost.**
>
> **Romans 14:17**

In the kingdom of God comes righteousness, which is the peace with God through the blood of Jesus Christ. There comes with that the peace of God, and with the peace of God comes joy in the Holy Spirit. When you don't have joy, look for the place where you lost your peace. Joy is the byproduct of the kingdom of God. If you are missing joy, somewhere you are missing the kingdom– in your marriage, your life and in your walk with God. One of the best witnesses we have to the world is joy and the second is peace. The world is always looking for joy and for peace. You cannot have joy until you have peace, and you cannot have peace until you have righteousness, which is the peace with God. Only then can you have the peace of God.

The peace of God is to rule in our hearts. The Greek word here for "rule" is the word for umpire, referee or to govern. It is the referee that judges to see if things are done right in a game, whether a baseball game, a football game or a basketball game. The umpire or the referee makes the call of the play. God wants you to listen to the Holy Spirit, who brings peace to your heart, and let Him become the umpire to call the balls and the strikes of your life. If He says safe, you can walk with confidence in what you are about to enter, knowing He is with you.

If the Holy Spirit is calling the situations and decisions that you are about to make or are making "out," and that you are not to press through, you are to let Him umpire or referee your life. It is a guidance system to protect you and not to put you in bondage, but instead to keep you out of bondage. The word "peace" comes from the Greek word "IREI." That is where we get the name Irene. It means in Greek "to join, to come into harmony or accord or agreement." The Hebrew word for peace is "SHALOM." This word carries a much greater and detailed meaning. In the Hebrew it is more than just the absence of strife. It means prosperity, happiness, success, security and safety. God wants these working in our lives.

Let us therefore follow after the things which make for peace, and things wherewith one may edify another.

Romans 14:19

Follow peace with all men, and holiness, without which no man shall see the Lord:

Hebrews 12:14

The Scripture says here that we should follow after those things that make for peace. What are those things? Harmony, security, prosperity, success and safety. God wants us to walk on these paths. When we follow peace, these are the paths we are following. In Hebrews 12 it says, "Follow peace with all men." Not just good men, all men. Not just the ones we like.

Satan has two weapons. The first is deception. The second is accusation. He will try to deceive you to feel good about that wrong decision you are about to make. Then when you do it, you lose your peace, and he accuses you. It is really double jeopardy. He sets you up through deception to do something wrong, then he accuses you for doing it. He will accuse you through the brethren. He will work in the Body of Christ through people, through the phone lines with murmuring and gossiping to create strife, confusion and accusations. Why? To rob you of your peace. He wants us to play into his hands no matter how well we were taught. You have to keep your righteousness intact. If the devil can shake your righteousness, you can lose your peace. The devil can rob the peace of God from a believer, but he cannot rob the peace with God from a believer, because Jesus accomplished it for us by His blood. The peace of God is only enjoyed as long as we are still before Him. We must shut out unbelief, strife, confusion and the world because God works in an atmosphere of peace.

THE REWARD OF THE PEACE OF GOD

There are three things the peace of God will do for you when you begin to walk in it. First, the peace of God will guide you. Second, the peace of God will govern and the peace of God will guard. In Romans 14:19, it says follow peace. In any decision, in any relationship or in any business deal, follow peace. If you are not feeling the peace, get off the road. You are on a wrong road. Peace is an umpire and it is to guide you into righteousness. We don't know everything, but the Holy Spirit does and we need to learn to obey the instructions that He has placed in us to navigate us.

> **And let the peace of God rule in your hearts, to the which also ye are called in one body; and be ye thankful.**
>
> **Colossians 3:15**

Second, the peace of God governs. In the above Scripture, it says let the peace of God rule or govern. God knows things that we don't know and He uses His peace to govern us.

> **Be careful for nothing; but in every thing by prayer and supplication with thanksgiving let your requests be made known unto God.**
>
> **Philippians 4:6**

Finally, the peace of God is a guard. In the above Scripture it says that the peace of God will guard, surround, and protect your hearts and minds through Christ Jesus. A strong warning is, be careful not to run through any stop signs of the peace of God. Obey it and let God have His way in your life.

> **And thou shalt go down before me to Gilgal; and, behold, I will come down unto thee, to offer burnt offerings, and to sacrifice sacrifices of peace offerings: seven days shalt thou tarry, till I come to thee, and shew thee what thou shalt do.**
>
> **I Samuel 10:8**

And the Philistines gathered themselves together to fight with Israel, thirty thousand chariots, and six thousand horsemen, and people as the sand which is on the sea shore in multitude: and they came up, and pitched in Michmash, eastward from Bethaven.

When the men of Israel saw that they were in a strait, (for the people were distressed,) then the people did hide themselves in caves, and in thickets, and in rocks, and in high places, and in pits.

And some of the Hebrews went over Jordan to the land of Gad and Gilead. As for Saul, he was yet in Gilgal, and all the people followed him trembling.

And he tarried seven days, according to the set time that Samuel had appointed: but Samuel came not to Gilgal; and the people were scattered from him.

And Saul said, Bring hither a burnt offering to me, and peace offerings. And he offered the burnt offering.

And it came to pass, that as soon as he had made an end of offering the burnt offering, behold, Samuel came; and Saul went out to meet him, that he might salute him.

And Samuel said, What hast thou done? And Saul said, Because I saw that the people were scattered from me, and that thou camest not within the days appointed, and that the Philistines gathered themselves together at Michmash;

I Samuel 13:5-11

Here in the Scripture, Saul was made the king of Israel. Samuel the prophet told him to wait seven days until he returned and he would offer to the Lord a sacrifice before they went into battle. Seven days went by, Samuel had not shown up and Saul was getting nervous. Stress was coming on him. He saw the enemy gathering, people joining other churches, and Samuel had not shown up. He got nervous and he violated the law of God which says only the priests can offer a sacrifice to the Lord. He did it under pressure and his peace was gone. He knew he was not supposed to do it and he violated his peace. As soon as he did it, Samuel showed up. Here is what Saul said to Samuel, "You did not come. The people were leaving. The enemy was gathering and I forced myself to make the offering." What does that mean? He violated the peace of God in his heart and he knew he was not supposed to do it. He should have said "I don't know God's plan, but I know that I am under authority. I don't know why Samuel has not shown up, but I am going to wait for God." There are many of us that will stand before choices and if we violate the peace of God, like Saul we will lose the kingdom. In the new covenant, the kingdom is righteousness, peace and joy.

GOD SPEAKING THROUGH GODLY COUNSEL

God also speaks to His people through counsels that are inspired by Him. God can direct and lead a believer through godly counsel. Often times the Body of Christ relies on two or three ways as the primary source by which God speaks to His people. God is not limited to one or two ways. We must rid ourselves of this mentality. The great danger of limiting God to only two ways is that the individual will become rigid, starchy and inflexible in their perception of God. When this state is reached, it is extremely difficult to hear, interpret or understand the leading of God. We must not just wait for God to speak to us through one way. We must be ready to receive His Word and act upon it when He speaks through Godly counsel.

> **Blessed, (happy, fortunate, prosperous and enviable) is the man who walks and lives not in the counsel of the**

ungodly (following their advice, their plans and purposes), nor stands (submissive and inactive) in the path where sinners walk, nor sits down (to relax and rest) where the scornful (and the mockers) gather.

But his delight and desire are in the law of the Lord, and on His law- the precepts, the instructions, the teachings of God-he habitually meditates (ponders and studies) by day and by night.

And he shall be like a tree firmly planted (and tended) by the streams of water, ready to bring forth his fruit in its season: his leaf also shall not fade or wither, and everything he does shall prosper (and come to maturity).

Psalms 1:1-4 (AMP)

From this Scripture, we can see that there are two types of counsel. The first is the counsel that proceeds out of the mouth of the godly and the second proceeds out of the mouth of the ungodly. The Bible lets us know that there are rewards attached to both the counsel of the godly and ungodly. A man that listens, accepts and walks in godly counsel enjoys the blessing of a happy, fortunate, prosperous and enviable life. But the opposite harvest awaits the man that follows the advice, plans and purposes of the ungodly. The godly man walks in the fear and love of God. He or she is kind, pious and reverential. An ungodly man is the opposite of a godly man.

The Scripture denotes the quality of a true godly man: he delights in the law of the Lord. He meditates in the law of God day and night. He is like a tree planted by the rivers of water. He brings forth fruit in his season. His leaf does not wither. He prospers in whatsoever he doeth. "The ungodly are not so." This is the kind of man that gives godly advice. Many times, believers run to the ungodly for advice. It is dangerous to be advised by an ungodly man. A godly man is accurate in his counsel. An ungodly man is very inaccurate.

> **The counsel of the LORD standeth for ever, the thoughts of his heart to all generations.**
>
> **Psalms 33:11**

The counsel that comes from God will stand the test of time. It will stand forever. When believers learn to listen and accept accurate counsel from godly men, doors of direction will open to them. There has been accurate counsel given by godly leaders that has been mistakenly rejected. Many look for God to speak in more sensational and spectacular channels than through godly counsel. Accurate counsel from a godly man is as God Himself speaking to an individual.

The Church needs guidance. We need some godly counsel from godly men. The Bible says that where there is no true counsel, the people fall. This is important. Many have fallen and missed the way because they refused to adhere to wise counsel. God is still speaking through men. Many visions, calls and lives have been destroyed because of the lack of guidance. Godly counsel brings protection and covering over anyone that will adhere to it.

> **Where there is no counsel, purposes are frustrated, but with many counselors they are accomplished.**
>
> **Proverbs 15:22 (AMP)**

The lack of giving and acceptance of godly counsel will frustrate your call, vision and purpose. Many believers have been frustrated and disappointed because they have not received wise counsel. A lot of Christians have aborted the plan of God for their lives because of a refusal to accept a true counsel from God. The Bible says that one that accepts true counsel is established. Wise counsel from God will establish you and set you in the right path with the right instructions.

CHAPTER VII

THE HINDRANCES TO HEARING THE VOICE OF GOD

God has an express goal in communication. He does nothing independent of divine purpose. God does not respond to begging. He does not respond to pressure and He certainly doesn't respond to need. God does not reveal Himself simply for the sake of revelation. When God reveals Himself, it is always deliberately. It is premeditated and divine destiny is always certain within it. There is an objective that God desires to communicate. God is not in the business of speaking just for the sake of hearing the sound of His Voice. He is deliberately seeking to reveal His character, His nature and His ways through His divine utterance.

Every word of God is pure: he is a shield unto them that put their trust in him.

Add thou not unto his words, lest he reprove thee, and thou be found a liar.

Proverbs 30:5-6

Ye shall not add unto the word which I command you, neither shall ye diminish ought from it, that ye may keep the commandments of the LORD your God which I command you.

Deuteronomy 4:2

For I testify unto every man that heareth the words of the prophecy of this book, If any man shall add unto these things, God shall add unto him the plagues that are written in this book:

And if any man shall take away from the words of the book of this prophecy, God shall take away his part out of the

book of life, and out of the holy city, and from the things which are written in this book.

Revelation 22:18-19

And this is the record, that God hath given to us eternal life, and this life is in his Son.

I John 5:11

If any man think himself to be a prophet, or spiritual, let him acknowledge that the things that I write unto you are the commandments of the Lord.

I Corinthians 14:37

Through the Scriptures, we see very clearly that God is concerned that His Word be conveyed and translated purely. God is concerned that every Word that comes forth out of His mouth stands upon itself and upon the laurels and power of His Presence that are contained within it. God does not want us to add to nor does He want us to take away from His Word. There is enough self-contained power within His Word to accomplish that which He has set it to accomplish. God has a divine purpose in communication. His purpose is for us to understand His truths.

Howbeit when he, the Spirit of truth, is come, he will guide you into all truth: for he shall not speak of himself; but whatsoever he shall hear, that shall he speak: and he will show you things to come.

John 16:13

There are some areas of truth that God is primarily interested in leading us into. The first area God is interested in is the truth concerning Himself. Paul cried out in Philippians 3:10, that he may know Christ and the power of

His resurrection and the fellowship of His sufferings. This was the embodiment of the cry of a man who desired to know God in His complete and His full revelation, not excluding any areas at all. God desires to reveal and communicate Himself to us.

The second area God is interested in is the truth about ourselves. Once you understand the truth about God, then you can begin to understand the truth about yourself.

Because of the redemptive value that is inherent in hearing the Voice of God, the enemy will do everything to stop or either restrict and pervert your ability to clearly hear the Voice of the Holy Spirit.

Therefore, we must be able to recognize the bondage, the hindrances and the restrictions that prevent us from hearing the Voice of God in our lives.

CARNALITY

The number one thing that restricts and resists the Voice of the Lord is carnality. We live in a society that dictates volumes to our minds. Our minds are geared to thinking in technological terms. We have children that are five and six years old that can operate video games equivalent to some of the airplancs we were flying twenty years ago. We have ten and twelve year olds that can function in computer science in ways that we don't even understand. They have been able to assimilate and accumulate information. We have never had a generation that had the wealth of information that is readily available as we have in this generation.

As a result of this, it has spilled over into the lifestyle of most Christians. Because we have to understand the microwave, and the compact disc player, and this appliance and that computer, we have become analytical and seek to understand the operation of the Holy Spirit through the same faculties.

There are some things contained in the nature of God, and there are some operations and manifestations contained in the outflow of the Holy Spirit, that you will never comprehend with your natural mind. You cannot understand the Holy Spirit, like you understand the computer. You cannot understand the Holy Spirit by just reading a manual. It is not an intellectual understanding that comes to us enabling us to comprehend Him, but it is a spiritual awakening.

Understanding the Voice of God is based on spiritual awakening, not intellectual understanding. There have been people that have little intellectual understanding, but they have great revelations. They have had a great spiritual awakening and they know how to interact and relate with the Holy Spirit, even though their natural learning was not up to the average ability.

> **For to be carnally minded is death; but to be spiritually minded is life and peace.**
>
> **Because the carnal mind is enmity against God: for it is not subject to the law of God, neither indeed can be.**
>
> **So then they that are in the flesh cannot please God.**
>
> **But ye are not in the flesh, but in the Spirit, if so be that the Spirit of God dwell in you. Now if any man have not the Spirit of Christ, he is none of his.**

And if Christ be in you, the body is dead because of sin; but the Spirit is life because of righteousness.

Romans 8:6-10

The biggest mistake you can ever make is to try and judge the things of the Spirit with the natural mind. The things of the Spirit cannot be naturally comprehended. The carnal mind will speak death. How can a man lay hands upon someone and something actually comes out of their hand that has healing in it? That is strange. But even though it is strange, only the spiritually minded person can comprehend it. How can we pray in intercession with groanings and travailings that really bring something to birth in the power of God? To the carnal mind, that is crazy and stupid. How can you stand and address a principality and power who you do not see, and who you have never seen, and who is supposed to be living over your city? These things are strange to the carnal mind. The carnal mind cannot assess it.

But there is something in us when the hand is laid upon us and the virtue is transferred into our body, and it creates a spiritual reawakening. We say that although we don't understand it, we do bear witness to it. There is something in you that recognizes the changes of the climate in a city, because principalities and powers are being dislodged. The carnal mind says "No," but the spirit man says "Yes." It brings revelation. It bears witness. The carnal mind does not and cannot understand the language of the spirit. The carnal mind is a foreigner and an alien when it comes to the things of the spirit. It does not have right of access which brings right of understanding. Therefore it cannot understand the language of the spirit.

Carnality stops the Voice of God. When you give in to carnality, it will restrict you from being able to hear God clearly. It will choke the precious fruit of the Holy Spirit in your life. Carnality will choke the sensitivity of God's Voice in your life. It will stop you from being spiritually adapted to hearing God's Voice.

UNBELIEF

> **And when he was come into his own country, he taught them in their synagogue, insomuch that they were astonished, and said, Whence hath this man this wisdom, and these mighty works?**
>
> **Is not this the carpenter's son? is not his mother called Mary? and his brethren, James, and Joses, and Simon, and Judas?**
>
> **And his sisters, are they not all with us? Whence then hath this man all these things?**
>
> **And they were offended in him. But Jesus said unto them, A prophet is not without honour, save in his own country, and in his own house.**
>
> **And he did not many mighty works there because of their unbelief.**
>
> **Matthew 13:54-58**

The second enemy or hindrance to hearing God's Voice is UNBELIEF. If you don't believe that the individual who brings forth a Word is called by God, then you will not be able to receive from him or hear the Voice of God speaking through him. The root of most Christian's inability to hear the Voice of God today is unbelief.

If you believe for yourself daily that God wants to interact with you, or if you believe for yourself daily that God wants to communicate with you, you have jumped a major hurdle in your Christian life. As long as the devil can sell you a bill of insecurity and say you are nothing, there is no reason that God will talk to you.

As long as the devil can sell you a bill of rejection, why would God want to talk to you? There is no need. You won't listen. He will talk to those that are around you. As long as the devil can deceive you, he will bring unbelief to you. Until you believe that it is His desire to speak, you will never begin to hear God's Voice speaking in your life. It is not that God is not speaking. He is still speaking. But the problem is that your unbelief has choked the Voice of God in your life. You have allowed the Voice of God to be drowned out in the multitude of crying unbelief. The screams and the echoes of doubt have choked the precious fruit of His Voice out of your life. Unbelief will stop you from hearing the Voice of God in your life. When you close your spiritual ears to the Voice of God, you become an echo. You are no longer a Voice.

DEEP REGARD FOR GOD'S WORD

All scripture is given by inspiration of God, and is profitable for doctrine, for reproof, for correction, for instruction in righteousness:

That the man of God may be perfect, thoroughly furnished unto all good works.

II Timothy 3:16-17

We need to have a deep regard for the Word of God in our personal value system. This will, in turn, prevent you from operating in unbelief. By studying and meditating on God's

Word consistently and daily, we can increase our understanding of God's vocabulary and gain knowledge of His Word and His ways. This will enable you to understand what God is saying and why He is saying it. In other words, the more we become familiar and acquainted with the Word of God, the easier we can discern when He is speaking.

> **Thy word have I hid in mine heart, that I might not sin against thee.**
>
> **Psalms 119:11**

There are no shortcuts to a meaningful relationship with God. Every believer is responsible to study the Word of God.

> **Therefore whosoever heareth these sayings of mine, and doeth them, I will liken him unto a wise man, which built his house upon a rock:**
>
> **And the rain descended, and the floods came, and the winds blew, and beat upon that house; and it fell not: for it was founded upon a rock.**
>
> **And every one that heareth these sayings of mine, and doeth them not, shall be likened unto a foolish man, which built his house upon the sand:**
>
> **And the rain descended, and the floods came, and the winds blew, and beat upon that house; and it fell: and great was the fall of it.**
>
> **Matthew 7:24-27**

In the parable of the two men who built houses, one on rock and the other on sand, both took the same amount of time to do the actual construction of their respective homes. The man who built his house on the sand could not say, "I did not have sufficient time to build my house on the rock." The question was not of time, but of treasure. The fact is that our perception of value will determine our priorities, which in turn will determine our practices. We only give time to what we value the most.

If we say we don't have time to read the Bible, we need to stop deceiving ourselves. The truth is that we do have the time, but we do not value the study of the Word enough to place priority upon it in our lives. This is a grave mistake to make because the storms of life are indiscriminate, periodically hammering us with the winds, pummeling us with rain and blasting us with floods, just as in the parable. By depriving ourselves of God's Word, we become increasingly disabled for the great challenges of life.

AN UNDEVELOPED SPIRIT MAN

The third hindrance that will shut up the Voice of God in your life is an undeveloped spirit man.

> **Of whom we have many things to say, and hard to be uttered, seeing ye are dull of hearing.**
>
> **For when for the time ye ought to be teachers, ye have need that one teach you again which be the first principles of the oracles of God; and are become such as have need of milk, and not of strong meat.**
>
> **For every one that useth milk is unskilful in the word of righteousness: for he is a babe.**
>
> **But strong meat belongeth to them that are of full age, even those who by reason of use have their senses exercised to discern both good and evil.**
>
> **Hebrews 5:11-14**

Just as you develop your physical man, you can also develop your spirit man. There are Christians that ought to be teachers, but they do not have enough of the Word in them and therefore are not developed in the things of the Spirit. Please understand this, you never outgrow milk. When the Scripture talks about using milk, it means using milk exclusively. If you have a spiritual diet of nothing more than milk, you are going to ultimately end up underdeveloped. As your diet progresses, to be able to handle meat or strong meat, you still must be able to receive a constant inflow of milk, of fluid, and of simple baby food.

Do you know what causes some Christians to seek for DEEP REVELATIONS and grow discontent with simple practical truths? Religious spirits. Some Christians cannot go to a church because it is too simple. They want some deep revelations. They want to hear about "the fourth angel that stands on the left side of Jesus." They want to flow with foolish genealogies and vain babbling. They end up with religious spirits that operate in vanity without substance. Our spiritual man needs to be developed so that we can be able to exercise our spiritual senses to discern between good and evil. Then your spiritual senses are fine-tuned and when this is done, you are developing your spirit man.

DECEPTION

The fourth hindrance to hearing the Voice of God is DECEPTION.

> **For we write none other things unto you, than what ye read or acknowledge; and I trust ye shall acknowledge even to the end;**

As also ye have acknowledged us in part, that we are your rejoicing, even as ye also are ours in the day of the Lord Jesus.

II Corinthians 1:13-14

Most Christians have learned to recognize deceptions in various manifestations. However most Christians do not clearly understand how to discern and recognize when the devil comes masquerading as an angel of light. When the enemy's tactics are open and clear, it is very easy to know that it is the devil and then something can be done. But that is not the same as when he shows up as an angel of light. One of the clearest ways that you can ever open yourself up for counterfeit words is to walk in a realm where you refuse to allow eldership in a local church to judge you. You put yourself in the position of constantly receiving words that cannot be verified.

It is dangerous to allow yourself to come into a position where you cannot be judged, whether you are a five-fold ministry gift, whether you are a governmental gift or a congregational gift.

Let the prophets speak two or three, and let the other judge.

I Corinthians 14:29

The Bible never said "Do not judge." We have greatly misunderstood what the Scriptures say about judgment. The Scripture simply says that if you are going to judge, be prepared to be judged with the same measure. There is a judgment that is exercised by the Spirit of God through eldership ministry in order to keep a true, pure flow of the Holy Spirit in operation.

In whom the God of this world hath blinded the minds of them which believe not, lest the light of the glorious gospel of Christ, who is the image of God, should shine unto them.

II Corinthians 4:4

The voice of deception always appeals to our flesh. Most deception is rooted in pride and in personal ambition. What is dangerous about deception is that when you are deceived, you won't even know that you are deceived. There is a spiritual element that is involved which will cloud your senses, judgment and ability to hear the Voice of the Holy Spirit with accuracy. Voices of deception operate most effectively in minds that have not been renewed according to the Word of God. When your mind is not renewed, you are open to deceptive Voices. The bottom line, when it comes to deception, is this: Does it violate God's Word in either letter or spirit? There are things that may not seem to violate God's Word and letter, but they violate God's Spirit. There is a difference in the Spirit of the Word and the Word itself. God expects them to be coupled together in our lives.

MEASURING THE VOICE THAT SPEAKS TO YOU

Ask yourself the question, "What does this Voice appeal to in my life? Does it just appeal to your mind, your will, or to your emotion? Is it appealing to your destiny? Is it appealing to your obedience, righteousness, holiness, sanctification?

WAYS DECEPTION ENTERS YOUR LIFE

The first way is through rebellion. When you rebel against the Word of God, you open the door to deception.

When you reject what God has to say through authority, you ultimately begin to hear what you want to hear. You'll hear it, then you'll believe it, and then you'll receive it. Now, you are deceived. That's why you see individuals running from one church to the other looking for a word to validate their deception. They run from one counselor to the next, and from one shepherd to the next. They're always looking for someone to validate what they want to hear. When you rebel against God's Voice, you ultimately have to find something to justify yourself. There will always be a deceptive voice to accommodate you in rebellion. There will always be a confirmation to be found somewhere.

The second way is by subjecting yourself to false teachers, false prophets, false apostles, and false doctrines. This will open you up to deception.

> **But evil men and seducers shall wax worse and worse, deceiving, and being deceived.**
>
> **II Timothy 3:13**

> **For the time will come when they will not endure sound doctrine; but after their own lusts shall they heap to themselves teachers, having itching ears;**
>
> **II Timothy 4:3**

> **That we henceforth be no more children, tossed to and fro, and carried about with every wind of doctrine, by the sleight of men, and cunning craftiness, whereby they lie in wait to deceive;**
>
> **Ephesians 4:14**

The third way is by causing offenses and divisions in the Body of Christ.

Now I beseech you, brethren, mark them which cause divisions and offences contrary to the doctrine which ye have learned; and avoid them.

For they that are such serve not our Lord Jesus Christ, but their own belly; and by good words and fair speeches deceive the hearts of the simple.

Romans 16:17-18

Their throat is an open sepulchre; with their tongues they have used deceit; the poison of asps is under their lips:

Whose mouth is full of cursing and bitterness:

Their feet are swift to shed blood:

Destruction and misery are in their ways:

And the way of peace have they not known:

There is no fear of God before their eyes.

Romans 3:13-18

If any man among you seem to be religious, and bridleth not his tongue, but deceiveth his own heart, this man's religion is vain.

James 1:26

Deception comes in a fourth manner through gossiping and malicious talk.

But be ye doers of the word, and not hearers only, deceiving your own selves.

James 1:22

Finally, hearing but not doing the Word of God gives entrance to spiritual deception. Deception will destroy you. It is not something to play with.

We must train ourselves to resist deception. How? Not by going out and studying every counterfeit spirit, but by knowing the Person of Truth. It is by walking with Truth. When you walk with Truth, you don't need to be afraid, because the Spirit of Truth is with you. When you come in contact with deception, you will easily discern the difference. Something in you tells you immediately that something is not right. It is the Voice of Truth within you.

The wolf also shall dwell with the lamb, and the leopard shall lie down with the kid; and the calf and the young lion and the fatling together; and a little child shall lead them.

Isaiah 11:6

God wants to develop us into a place where we become quick of understanding. God wants us to be so quick of understanding that when we come in contact with deception, we don't even need to go pray, fast and meditate about it. We just know and understand that it is deception. Daily we need to quote this Scripture in Isaiah, "....the promise of God to make us of a quick understanding in the fear of the Lord."

A HEARING EAR

The heart of the prudent getteth knowledge; and the ear of the wise seeketh knowledge.

Proverbs 18:15

In the Bible we find the expression, "He that has an ear, let him hear." This does not refer to the ears on the sides of our heads, but to the ears within our hearts. The prayer of the Scripture is that the eyes of our understanding of our heart would be open that we might see the things of God.

That the God of our Lord Jesus Christ, the Father of glory, may give unto you the spirit of wisdom and revelation in the knowledge of him:

The eyes of your understanding being enlightened; that ye may know what is the hope of his calling, and what the riches of the glory of his inheritance in the saints,

And what is the exceeding greatness of his power to us-ward who believe, according to the working of his mighty power,

Which he wrought in Christ, when he raised him from the dead, and set him at his own right hand in the heavenly places,

Ephesians 1:17-20

The Lord GOD hath given me the tongue of the learned, that I should know how to speak a word in season to him that is weary: he wakeneth morning by morning, he wakeneth mine ear to hear as the learned.

Isaiah 50:4

When is a hearing ear given to us? A hearing ear is given to each of us when we are born again. Now, although the capacity to hear the Lord is present, we must develop the ability to do so.

Another hindrance to your hearing the Voice of God is the spirit of deafness.

> **And in them is fulfilled the prophecy of Esaias, which saith, By hearing ye shall hear, and shall not understand; and seeing ye shall see, and shall not perceive:**
>
> **For this people's heart is waxed gross, and their ears are dull of hearing, and their eyes they have closed; lest at any time they should see with their eyes and hear with their ears, and should understand with their heart, and should be converted, and I should heal them.**
>
> **But blessed are your eyes, for they see: and your ears, for they hear.**
>
> **For verily I say unto you, That many prophets and righteous men have desired to see those things which ye see, and have not seen them; and to hear those things which ye hear, and have not heard them.**
>
> **Matthew 13:14-17**
>
> **Seeing then that we have such hope, we use great plainness of speech:**
>
> **II Corinthians 3:12**

These are door openers to deafness. Hurts open the door to deafness. Unforgiveness, jealousy and an unhealthy fear open the door to deafness. Evil spirits can also open the door to deafness.

I say the truth in Christ, I lie not, my conscience also bearing me witness in the Holy Ghost,

Romans 9:1

This sixth hindrance to the Voice of God is a callous conscience. Every man has been given the power of conscience. Our body speaks to us through feelings. Our soul speaks to us through thoughts and our spirit speaks to us through conscience. Believers and unbelievers alike have a conscience. There is something within them that communicates to them. Your conscience is usually formed by your environment. That is why one person's conscience will be offended in one area and another person's will not. To the one that has grown up in an ungodly atmosphere, they will have to begin to develop their conscience by the Word of God. The revelation of the Word will purge their conscience.

I charge thee therefore before God, and the Lord Jesus Christ, who shall judge the quick and the dead at his appearing and his kingdom;

Preach the word; be instant in season, out of season; reprove, rebuke, exhort with all longsuffering and doctrine.

II Timothy 4:1-2

A conscience can be seared so that you cannot hear the expression of the Holy Spirit.

HARBORING SIN

Another hindrance to hearing the Voice of God is harboring sin. Harboring sin is different from committing sin. Harboring sin is refusing to deal with an area that God through His Spirit has exposed. It is the intentional forming of walls to hide your sin, pretending that God does not see it by lying to yourself and creating excuses for why you do what you do, and why it is okay to do what you do. Those harboring sin will destroy the life in your spirit man.

Blessed are the pure in heart: for they shall see God.

Matthew 5:8

Unto the pure all things are pure: but unto them that are defiled and unbelieving is nothing pure; but even their mind and conscience is defiled.

Titus 1:15

We must learn to turn to the Lord for cleansing whenever we are defiled. Otherwise, we will carry the defilement within our hearts and find ourselves unable to receive when God speaks. A wounded heart can distort a good signal. The signal from the radio is perfectly clear, but the message being heard in the living room is garbled and irritated.

ANGER

Another hindrance is anger.

But if ye have bitter envying and strife in your hearts, glory not, and lie not against the truth.

This wisdom descendeth not from above, but is earthly, sensual, devilish.

For where envying and strife is, there is confusion and every evil work.

James 3:14-16

When strife comes into our heart and anger is manifested, it is an affront to truth. When anger is involved, truth becomes confused and the Voice of God becomes distorted. Proper judgment becomes distorted. The water becomes muddy. In the heart of passionate anger, truth cannot be recognized. Anger silences the Voice of God.

There are many types of anger. There is the anger against God or a God-directed anger. This is when you cannot hear God because you are angry against Him. It is surprising that we have a lot of Christians that are angry with God because of the loss of their loved ones or because what they ask for or are believing for has not yet come to pass. Some Christians have been told that God took the life of their only child, the life of their wife, the life of their lovely husband or parents. Because of a false image about God being erected in their minds, they are angry with God which makes it impossible for them to hear the Voice of God to discern what He is saying and where He is leading them.

The second kind of anger is the self-inflicted anger. This is when you are unable to hear your own conscience because you are angry with yourself. This is when you hate yourself, feel stupid and feel lowly, and also feel that all the decisions you make are all dumb. This anger then shuts up the Voice of your conscience.

The third kind of anger is directed at others. You are angry at other people. This hinders your prayers. And if prayer is supposed to be a communication between you and God, that means that you can try to communicate, but there will be no response.

A REBELLIOUS SPIRIT

A rebellious spirit will also prevent you from hearing the Voice of God.

> **For rebellion is as the sin of witchcraft, and stubbornness is as iniquity and idolatry. Because thou hast rejected the word of the LORD, he hath also rejected thee from being king.**
>
> **I Samuel 15:23**

Do you know that rebellion is not the same as reluctance? There is a difference between reluctance and rebellion. Reluctance is something that God wants to deal with in us, so that we are completely trustworthy. But an individual may be dealing with reluctance because they don't fully trust the Voice of God in their lives. There is a difference between that and someone who resists the Voice of God in their lives due to rebellion. Rebellion is as the sin of witchcraft. Reluctance will be worked through as you learn to trust God, and as you learn to step out by faith and obey that which God directs you to do.

Pride is always the root of all rebellion. When rebellion is manifested, it is nothing more than an offshoot of pride, self will and independence. It is the "I will" attitude. If you can conquer the root of pride, rebellion is then not much to deal with.

THE MESSENGERS OF GOD

The final hindrance is the rejection of God's messengers.

And the LORD said unto Samuel, Hearken unto the voice of the people in all that they say unto thee: for they have not rejected thee, but they have rejected me, that I should not reign over them.

I Samuel 8:7

Israel cried out for a king. They wanted a king in order to be like the other neighboring nations. God told them that kingship was not in their best interest. Yet the children of Israel persisted and wanted their own way. Despite God's recommendation, they still remained persistent with their demand for a king. Rejecting God's messengers, rejects the Voice of God. An individual who is rebellious shuts off the standard of authority in their life.

When you reject God's messengers, you shut off the standard of authority. Suddenly, every man begins to do that which is right in his own eyes. You have invalidated God's authority, and criticism and fault finding begin to consume your thoughts. The prideful, independent spirit of rebellion knows that if he can invalidate the man, he can invalidate the message. That is why God's prophets are often slaughtered for what they preach. John the Baptist had his head taken off because of his message. The end of a critical spirit is the destruction of trustworthiness and confidence.

The end of accusation, and the end of rejecting God's messenger signals the destruction of our lives. This brings division, isolation and great loneliness. God wants to speak to us. But in order for Him to speak effectively and for us to hear Him, we must make sure that we avoid these hindrances.

HOW TO DIFFERENTIATE THE VOICE OF GOD FROM THE VOICE OF THE ENEMY

My sheep hear my voice, and I know them, and they follow me:

And I give unto them eternal life; and they shall never perish, neither shall any man pluck them out of my hand.

My Father, which gave them me, is greater than all; and no man is able to pluck them out of my Father's hand.

I and my Father are one.

John 10:27-30

And when they shall say unto you, Seek unto them that have familiar spirits, and unto wizards that peep, and that mutter: should not a people seek unto their God? for the living to the dead?

Isaiah 8:19

First, does the Voice line up with the Word of God? Does it line up with God's attitude? Does it line up with His expression? If an idea, an inclination, or a suggestion comes to you that does not agree with the Word of God, then it does not line up with God.

There are many devices in a man's heart; nevertheless the counsel of the LORD, that shall stand.

Proverbs 19:21

Second, how does the Voice feel when being tested by eldership? Ask that Voice, "Hey, what do you think if I go to ask some elder or some leader in the church that flows and understands the leading of the Spirit?" How does it respond when you desire to have it tested? If it is a Voice from God, it will stand the test. Child of God, listen to me, if it is God, it will stand the test of eldership. If you are truly healed, you go to the doctor for verification, your healing will stand the scrutiny of the medical doctor who will be forced to verify your miracle. Any voice that resents the scrutiny of authority is a voice that does not proceed from God.

> **Beloved, believe not every spirit, but try the spirits whether they are of God: because many false prophets are gone out into the world.**
>
> **Hereby know ye the Spirit of God: Every spirit that confesseth that Jesus Christ is come in the flesh is of God:**
>
> **And every spirit that confesseth not that Jesus Christ is come in the flesh is not of God: and this is that spirit of antichrist, whereof ye have heard that it should come; and even now already is it in the world.**
>
> **I John 4:1-3**

Third, it will always exhort Jesus. When God speaks to you concerning a plan, a direction or a decision, those plans, those decisions and those directions will always exhort Jesus when they are done.

> **The Spirit itself beareth witness with our spirit, that we are the children of God:**
>
> **Romans 8:16**

Fourth, the Holy Spirit will confirm and bear witness to God's directions. When God speaks to you, the Holy Spirit will place His stamp of approval upon it.

Because thou sayest, I am rich, and increased with goods, and have need of nothing; and knowest not that thou art wretched, and miserable, and poor, and blind, and naked:

Revelation 3:17

Now when they had gone throughout Phrygia and the region of Galatia, and were forbidden of the Holy Ghost to preach the word in Asia,

After they were come to Mysia, they assayed to go into Bithynia: but the Spirit suffered them not.

And they passing by Mysia came down to Troas.

And a vision appeared to Paul in the night; There stood a man of Macedonia, and prayed him, saying, Come over into Macedonia, and help us.

Acts 16:6-9

Fifth, when God speaks to you concerning a thing, He will always open doors for you. Paul and his people wanted to go to Asia, but God stopped them and told them not to go. In verse 9, God opened doors for them to preach in Macedonia. Now, listen very carefully. Just because a door is open, does not mean it is God's will. You must check it from the beginning to the end to make sure that it lines up with the Word.

Finally, will the consequences of obeying that Voice ultimately produce life or death? Can you stop and look down the road far enough ahead in the future to see whether or not the consequences of obeying that Voice will produce life or death?

To request a complete catalog featuring books, video and audio tapes by Dr. John Tetsola, or to contact him for speaking engagements, please write or call:

Ecclesia Word Ministries International
P.O. Box 743
Bronx, New York 10462

(718) 904-8530